Graphis Inc. is committed to presenting exceptional work in international Design, Advertising, Illustration & Photography.

Where do ideas come from?

**Published by Graphis | Publisher & Creative Director: B. Martin Pedersen | Design: Jimin Nam | Editor: Annemarie McNamara
Production: Linh Truong | Executive Assistant: Sara Allen**

LET

"Contemporary culture
places an unfortunate emphasis
on"knowing what you want"
and, of course, "being smart."
Unfortunately this works against
the design process."

GO

Contents

Previous spread: Design Month by David Schwen | *Opposite page:* UNEXPECT: The Works of Michael Ryan Architects by Justin LaFontaine

In Memoriam

Al Ross
Cartoonist
1912 – 2012
United States

Ben Van Os
Art Director
1945 – 2012
United States

Blaine
Editorial Cartoonist
1938 – 2012
Canada

Carolyn Autry
Artist & Printmaker
1914 – 2012
United States

Donald Takayama
Surf Board Designer
1944 – 2012
United States

Eddy Paape
Graphic Designer
1934 – 2009
Finland

Ernie Chan
Comic Artist
1921 – 2012
United States

Fran Materea
Comic Strip Artist
1929 – 2012
United States

Hillman Curtis
Director & Designer
1961 – 2012
United States

Himanish Goswami
Cartoonist
1927 – 2012
United States

Ib Spang Olsen
Cartoonist
1922 – 2012
Denmark

J. Michael Riva
Production Desginer
1949 – 2012
United States

Jackie McAllister
Curator & Artist
1963 – 2012
United States

Jean Giraud
Comic-book Artist
1939 – 2012
France

Joe Kubert
Comic Book Artist
1927 – 2012
United States

John Celardo
Comic Strip Artist
1919 – 2012
United States

John Griffiths
Illustrator
1927 – 2012
Britain

John Severin
Comic Book Artist
1922 – 2012
United States

Laura A. Minchella
Graphic Designer
1934 – 2009
Finland

Leo Dillon
Comic Book Artist
1933 – 2012
United States

Leonard Rosoman
Painter & Graphic Artist
1914 – 2012
Britain

LeRoy Neiman
Artist & Illustrator
1921 – 2012
United States

Malcolm Fowler
Artist & Designer
1944 – 2012
London

Marc Swayze
Comic Book Artist
1913 – 2012
United States

Marilyn Houlberg
Artist & Illustrator
1940 – 2012
United States

Mario Armond Zamparelli
Design Artist
1921 – 2012
United States

Maurice Sendak
Illustrator & Author
1929 – 2012
United States

Michael Asher
Conceptual Artist
1943 – 2012
United States

Paul Rudall
Artist & Illustrator
1921 – 2012
Britain

Ralph McQuarrie
Designer
1930 – 2012
United States

Rex Babin
Cartoonist
1963 – 2012
United States

Sergio Toppi
Cartoonist
1933 – 2012
Italy

Sheldon Moldoff
Comic Book Artist
1921 – 2012
United States

Sid Couchey
Comic Book Artist
1920 – 2012
United States

Themo Lobos
Comic Book Artist & Writer
1929 – 2012
Chile

William Moggridge
Designer & Educator
1943 – 2012
Britain

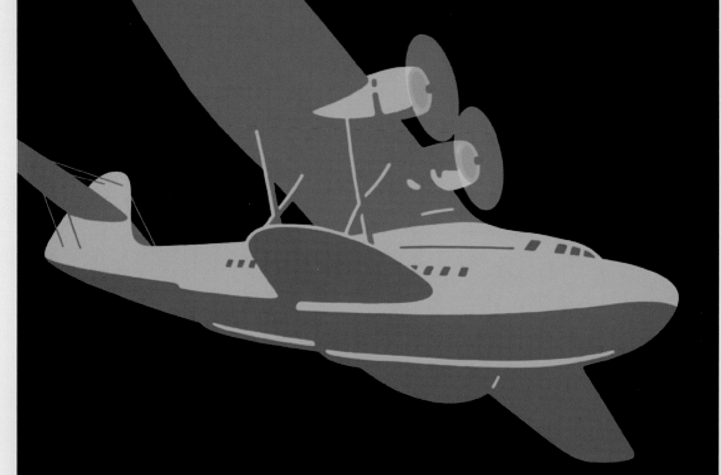

DREAMS
AND
DESTINATIONS

THE GLAMOUR OF
ESCAPE

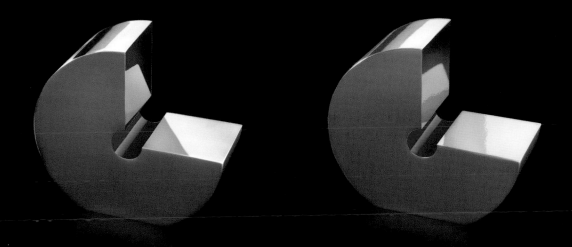

PlatinumWinners

pg. 84 / Category: Catalogues
Title: Lida Baday Fall/Winter 2011 Brochure
Designers: Melatan Riden, Leticia Luna
Design Firm: Concrete Design Communications
Creative Directors: Diti Katona, John Pylypczak / Client: Lida Baday

pg. 110 / Category: Editorial / Title: Burning Man
Designer: Benjamin Bours / Design Firm: GQ Magazine / Client: GQ Magazine

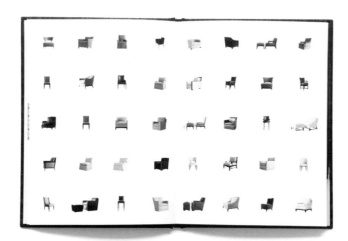

pg. 72 / Category: Brochures / Title: A.Rudin Product Overview Book /
Designers: Kellie McCool, Michael Vanderbyl / Design Firm: Vanderbyl Design
Creative Director: Michael Vanderbyl / Client: A. Rudin

pg. 198 / Category: Posters / Title: AS IF Magazine
Designers: Toshiaki Ide, Hisa Ide / Design Firm: IF Studio
Photographer: Tatijana Shoan / Client: AS IF Magazine

pg. 180 / Category: Packaging / Title: Balla
Designers: Vince Frost, Graziela Machado
Design Firm: Frost* Design / Client: Manfredi

pg. 118 / Category: Editorial / Title: Proud Editorial Design
Designer: Osamu Misawa / Design Firm: omdr design agency
Client: Nomura Real Estate Development Co., Ltd.

pg 140 / Category: Exhibits / Title: Think / Design Firm: Ralph Appelbaum Associates / Client: IBM

pg 80 / Category: Calendars / Title: Past and Future / Designer: Eduardo Aires / Design Firm: White Studio / Client: Bitri

Assignment: SL Green wanted its annual report to communicate to its stakeholders the key long-term attributes that contribute to SL Green's success story in Manhattan's commercial real estate space. The company wanted to showcase its trophy assets as well as outline its growth strategy. The report also had to express the heart of the story, which is SL Green's experience and innovative ability to create value in multiple ways due to a fundamental understanding of operating in its market.

Approach: Starting with the theme of "Setting the Bar," we divide the report into five chapters to outline each of the ways SL Green does just that. The report reads as a list of essential "ingredients" to SL Green's success. We open by leveraging the highly visual—and tangible—trophy assets as an entry point to the conversation about the intangible strategies and activities that create value for the company and its shareholders. The report then offers an inside glimpse to the company and its key relationships. Each chapter is deliberately treated in a very different way, but a thread of visual consistency remains throughout the piece. The final takeaway is the collection of unparalleled attributes, which together result in SL Green's ability to continually create value in Manhattan's commercial real estate space.

Results: Early on, the client reacted very well to the list-of-five approach as a way of laying out their value proposition. Then, in terms of design and production, the client felt that the piece succeeded as a premium showcase for the company.

Designers: Rick Slusher, Glenn Chan | **Design Firm:** Addison | **Client:** SL Green Realty Corp.

SL GREEN
REALTY CORP.

2011 Annual Report

Our solid financial position is derived by a carefully managed balance sheet with exceptional liquidity—underpinned by deep relationships with global capital providers, including Bank of China, to New York City, one of the strongest, most desirable commercial real estate markets in the world. Our financial fortitude is proven. We successfully maneuvered through the last recession and we've come out stronger, continuing to thrive with an ambitious investment strategy that takes full advantage of the market recovery. With our well-primed balance sheet supporting our ability to execute, we will continue capitalizing on value-add opportunities when they arise.

Shown here: Fifteen Fifteen Broadway

Our strong capacity for unsecured borrowings is enhanced by a collection of high-quality New York City and suburban office properties that are unencumbered by any debt. Among them are premier properties such as 1185 Avenue of the Americas, which is home to the National Hockey League's headquarters, the Hess Corporation's headquarters and international law firm King & Spalding LLP and 360 Hamilton Avenue in White Plains, New York.

Shown here: Eleven Eighty Five Avenue of the Americas

SETTING THE BAR

ENERGY. AMBITION. INGENUITY. OPPORTUNITY. TRADEMARKS OF NEW YORK CITY—ONE OF THE LEADING COMMERCIAL OFFICE MARKETS IN THE WORLD. HAVING A DISTINCT POINT OF VIEW, IMPLEMENTING STRATEGIES, DEVELOPING KEY RELATIONSHIPS AND UTILIZING OUR TEAMS' UNMATCHED SKILL SET. SL GREEN TURNS IDEAS INTO REALITY—CREATING VALUE FOR OUR SHAREHOLDERS. EXECUTION. DEDICATION. DETERMINATION. SL GREEN SETS THE BAR.

THE PORTFOLIO

THREE COLUMBUS CIRCLE

Scale. Quality. Market Penetration. SL Green's Manhattan portfolio is unrivaled. Our asset profile is strong and durable—and we invest substantial effort and capital to keep it that way—reaping the rewards with an average Manhattan portfolio occupancy of 96% since 1993 and consistently outperforming the market. The SL Green investment portfolio encompasses 45 million square feet—equivalent in size to the 5th largest CBD in the United States—with ownership interests in 27 million square feet of premier urban office and retail properties, our 6 million square foot suburban office portfolio, debt and preferred equity investments secured by nearly 12 million square feet, and with recently acquired residential assets.

THE BALANCE SHEET

With a strong balance sheet, we enjoy continual demand from providers of capital to lend and invest in our premier Manhattan and suburban portfolios—giving us flexible financial options and cost of capital advantages. During 2011, this translated to efficient financing for $4.4 billion of real estate investments. We demonstrated our breadth of access by financing our growth with equity raised through joint ventures, sales of assets, and public issuances of common stock, supplemented with mortgage debt, and an issuance in the unsecured bond markets. S&P awarded us with our first BBB- investment grade rating during the year, and we used that rating along with our deep lender relationships to refinance our $1.5 billion revolving line of credit with 26 of the world's most sophisticated and highest credit quality lenders.

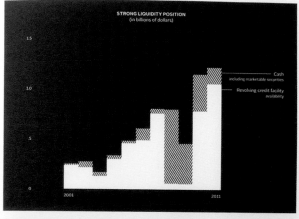

STRONG LIQUIDITY POSITION
(in billions of dollars)

Cash
including marketable securities

Revolving credit facility
availability

2001 — 2011

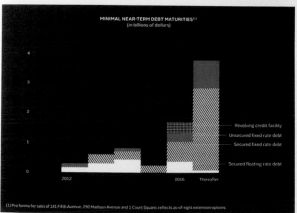

MINIMAL NEAR-TERM DEBT MATURITIES[1]
(in billions of dollars)

Revolving credit facility

Unsecured fixed rate debt

Secured fixed rate debt

Secured floating rate debt

2012 — 2016 — Thereafter

(1) Pro forma for sales of 141 Fifth Avenue, 292 Madison Avenue and 1 Court Square; reflects as-of-right extension options.

Assignment: The objective of this piece was to showcase Neenah Paper brands and explain the business in terms of competitive advantage and opportunities. We needed to express Neenah's ability to manufacture specialized and premium products, as well as to communicate the value and benefit of being niche-focused.

Approach: So many markets, applications, and end uses are touched by Neenah's products. We started with that. This is expressed first through a wrap-around dust jacket that unfolds to reveal a poster-size illustration of the rare and exotic ways the paper is used in the world. That message is furthered by information graphics inside. The idea of Neenah's niche focus inspired the abstract foil-stamped shapes opening each section. The theme, "We make paper that makes its way into many things," also informs the unique grid elements and intertwined display typography throughout. The piece utilizes high-quality art and production techniques, and leverages the format as an opportunity to differentiate and engage. This is an annual report that only Neenah Paper could issue.

Results: The dust jacket and product-centric narrative were especially well-received.

Designer: Jason Miller | **Design Firm:** Addison | **Client:** Neenah Paper, Inc.

PART I: STRATEGIC REVIEW

Building on our strengths in diverse products,
markets and regions

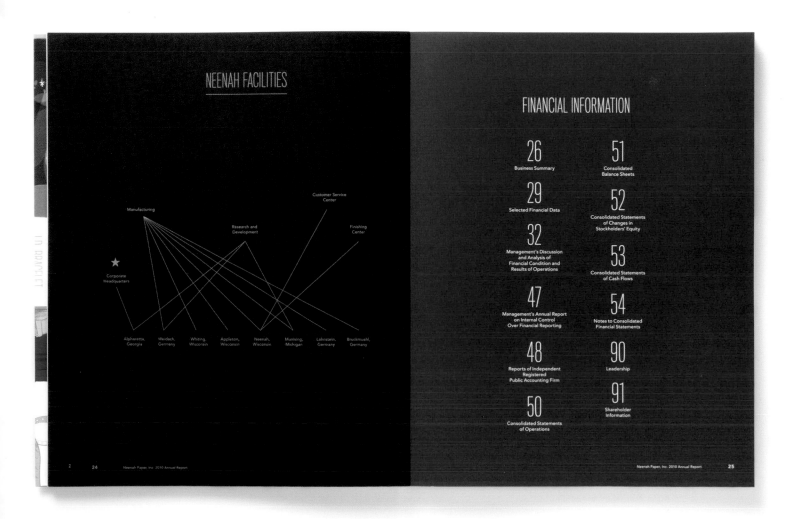

NEENAH FACILITIES

★ Corporate
Headquarters

Manufacturing

Research and
Development

Customer Service
Center

Finishing
Center

Alpharetta,
Georgia

Weidach,
Germany

Whiting,
Wisconsin

Appleton,
Wisconsin

Neenah,
Wisconsin

Munising,
Michigan

Lahnstein,
Germany

Bruckmuehl,
Germany

FINANCIAL INFORMATION

Assignment: Our assignment was to design an Annual Report for Celtic Exploration. The key message that Celtic wanted to get across was that through perseverance, patience, progression, and preparedness the company was able to springboard into 2012 and capitalize on their world-class assets.

Sub-message: Celtic has liquid-rich resource plays and is a leader in its sector.

Objectives and goals:

1) Show what sets Celtic apart from its competitors,

2) through clear and concise messaging, and

3) abstaining from fancy printing techniques.

Approach: The theme for the Annual Report was "Defining Celtic," so we used infographics to showcase what differentiates Celtic from its competitors. We wanted the annual to be simple yet engaging, so we let the numbers speak for themselves and designed the report with only two colors. The goal was to highlight Celtic's virtues of perseverance and patience and let the strengths of the company shine through visual experiences.

Results: The response was great and the client loved it. The annual has won a vast array of awards, including being published in *Coupe Magazine,* ranked #25 in their Design and Image Annual.

Designer: Jake Lim | **Design Firm:** Foundry Communications | **Client:** Celtic Exploration

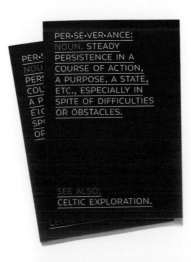

Percentage of 2010 Production

North East British Columbia
Inga
—

Northern Alberta
Utikuma
1%

West Central Alberta
Kaybob, Fir, Resthaven
92%

East Central Alberta
Ashmont, Edward
1%

Southern Alberta
Drumheller, Michichi, Princess, Bantry
6%

Gas Properties

Oil Properties

RESOURCE PLAYS HAVE CHANGED THE LANDSCAPE OF THE WESTERN CANADIAN SEDIMENTARY BASIN WHICH WAS PREVIOUSLY VIEWED AS MATURE WITH LIMITED GROWTH OPPORTUNITIES.

NET ACRES OF UNDEVELOPED LAND AT DECEMBER 31, 2010: 621,199 / NET WELLS DRILLED IN 2010: 41.9 / NET DRILLING SUCCESS RATE IN 2010: 90% / PERCENTAGE INCREASE IN PROVED PLUS PROBABLE RESERVES IN 2010: 12%

Horizontal drilling techniques with completions using multi-stage fractures have created opportunities to unlock significant hydrocarbon reservoirs that were previously inaccessible.

Celtic has been a leader using horizontal drilling with multi-stage completions at Kaybob in the Triassic Montney and Cretaceous Bluesky and Notikewin formations. In 2011, Celtic expects to apply its knowledge and experience with exploration at Resthaven in the Triassic Montney and at Kaybob in the Devonian Duvernay, with the objective of ultimately adding new resource plays to the Company's asset base. After drilling numerous wells, Celtic has gained sufficient experience to drill in the most efficient manner, reducing capital costs, ultimately leading to lower finding costs. Examples are the use of multi-pad drilling locations and longer horizontal laterals with a large number of fractures.

Celtic's Montney and Bluesky prospects at Kaybob would have been categorized as conventional reservoirs in the past. However, new technology allows the Company to provide repeatable drilling results and higher recovery rates of gas-in-place, ultimately leading to long-life production categorized as resource plays.

Maintaining Confidence — Production Growth

Since Celtic's first full calendar year of operations in 2003, production has grown at a compound annual growth rate ("CAGR") of 37% from 1,941 BOE per day in 2003 to 17,304 BOE per day in 2010. On a per share basis, production has grown at a CAGR of 24% from 2003 to 2010. Over 80% of the production in 2010 has come from organic growth and the remainder from strategic acquisitions.

Production per Million Shares (BOE/d):

Year	Value
2010	193
2009	163
2008	138
2007	111
2006	97
2005	79
2004	70
2003	44

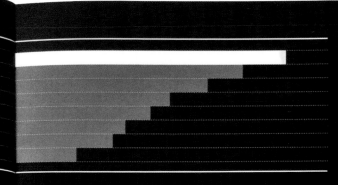

37%	24%	791%	17,304
CAGR in production from 2003 to 2010	CAGR in production per share from 2003 to 2010	Growth in production from 2003 to 2010	2010 average daily production

35%	25%	735%	$930,750
CAGR in reserves from 2003 to 2010	CAGR in reserves per share from 2003 to 2010	Growth in reserves from December 2003 to December 2010	NPV of reserves discounted at 10% BT, as at December 31, 2010 ($ thousands)

Operational Excellence — Reserves Growth

Since December 31, 2003, after Celtic's first full calendar year of operations, reserves have grown at a CAGR of 35% from 8.1 million BOE at December 31, 2003 to 67.5 million BOE at December 31, 2010. On a per share basis, reserves have grown at a CAGR of 25% from December 31, 2003 to December 31, 2010. At December 31, 2010, the net present value of proved plus probable reserves, discounted at 10% before tax, was $0.9 billion, using forecasted 2011 average commodity prices of US$88.40 per barrel for WTI oil and $3.83 per GJ for AECO gas. Celtic's net reserve additions in 2010 replaced production in the year by a factor of 2.1 times.

2P Reserves per thousand Shares (BOE):

Year	Value
2010	743
2009	678
2008	649
2007	448
2006	409
2005	319
2004	214
2003	157

Assignment: BlackRock sought to tie-in the company's new strategic brand and advertising program with their annual report.

Approach: Decker Design's approach began with exploring ways to create graphics that integrate with the new brand and advertising campaign. We arrived at the concept by creating a ticker tape with important data points, and using images of employees and colorful graphics throughout the book.

Designers: Michael Aron, Susanne Adrian, Bradley Cushing | **Design Firm:** Decker Design | **Client:** BlackRock

BLACKROCK

BLK

Assignment: MiresBall designed this keepsake book celebrating the authenticity and passion of the Shure brand.

Designer: Angela Renac | **Design Firm:** MiresBall | **Creative Director:** John Ball | **Copywriter:** David Fried | **Account Supervisor:** Holly Houk
Photographers: Jeffrey Brown, Lou Mora, Marc Tule, Chris Wimpey, Bil Zelman | **Client:** Shure

LEGENDARY PERFORMANCE

Assignment: Art Center College of Design, located in Pasadena, California, is one of the world's leading design schools. DOT Launch is the school's new entrepreneurial initiative dedicated to empowering design entrepreneurs by providing enterprising Art Center designers with the knowledge, experience, and resources needed to develop new entrepreneurial opportunities and models. Our assignment was to create a unique, memorable, and compelling branding program that would clearly communicate the DOT Launch mission, connect the entrepreneurial initiative to the school, and resonate with Art Center students, faculty, and alumni.

Approach: Art Center College of Design is known for its orange dot symbol. Our design strategy was to use the orange dot to connect the entrepreneurial initiative to the school and convey the initiative's mission. The logo, tagline, and secondary symbols are used in a strategic manner to create a cohesive and comprehensive program. Each application of the brand sought to further the ideas and objectives of the entrepreneurial initiative. The DOT Launch logo uses the orange dot to connect the initiative to the school. The soaring rocket metaphor symbolizes the launch of new enterprises and innovative businesses achieving liftoff. The logo also creates a symbolic pencil point, since many great design concepts originate with a simple pencil sketch. The tagline clearly defines the initiative's focus, identifies its audience, and reinforces the launch theme. The logo can be used in a number of different signature configurations to meet a variety of space requirements, resulting in an extremely flexible branding system. The animated intro connects the rocket launch to a pencil point as the genesis for innovative design ideas. The secondary symbol system places Art Center's orange dot at the center of each of the entrepreneurial initiative's core aspirations. The business card creates a rocket exhaust trail with its typography. The T-shirt uses a striking black background to introduce the brand. The award recognizes Partners, Mentors, and Entrepreneurs, using the logo to create a unique dimensional form.

Results: The response to the DOT Launch branding program from its target audience of students, alumni, faculty, and partners has been overwhelmingly positive. The program has spurred participation from students in mentorship and licensing, mentoring by alumni, engagement from faculty, and collaboration with partners. Most important, the DOT Launch is helping to change the way educational institutions teach, mentor, and inspire design entrepreneurs. In doing so, the DOT Launch branding program has played an important role in placing Art Center at the forefront of educational efforts to successfully integrate design and entrepreneurship.

Designer: Earl Gee | **Design Firm:** Gee + Chung Design | **Client:** Art Center College of Design

DOT LAUNCH
2012 MENTOR
JOE TAN
INCASE

Assignment: Pregnancy is a temporary period of time in a woman's life, although, as many women have told me, it can seem to go on forever. A pregnant woman's body undergoes a remarkable change that, to me, imparts a sculptural quality to her form. I felt that this anatomical and physiological change, especially in the last weeks of pregnancy, had the potential for powerful imagery. When I began the project, I initially contacted obstetricians, pediatricians, and midwives. Many were helpful and referred pregnant women to me. The fact that I was a physician may well have helped at this early stage of the project. After a while, I began to hear from women who had been told about the project by a friend whom I'd photographed, or by someone who had seen images on our Web site. We made contact with a modeling agency that specialized in pregnant models. We put notices up at professional dance company studios all over New York. We even got calls from dancers and fashion models I had photographed for other projects who were now expecting a first child.

Approach: The challenge in making images for this project was to "see" pregnancy in every way that I could, and to attempt to capture the sculptural quality of women, to use an apt Biblical term, "great with child." At the end of every session, I asked each woman to return with her new baby so that I could make a photograph of the two of them. The special bond of mother and newborn child gave me a unique opportunity to make what I hope are very moving images.

Results: This was a personal explorative, artistic endeavor. Sales of the book were and continue to be very successful. The book, *with Child,* is readily available, and there have been a number of gallery exhibitions with sales of fine art prints.

Designer: Howard Schatz | **Design Firm:** Schatz Ornstein Studio | **Client:** Glitterati Incorporated

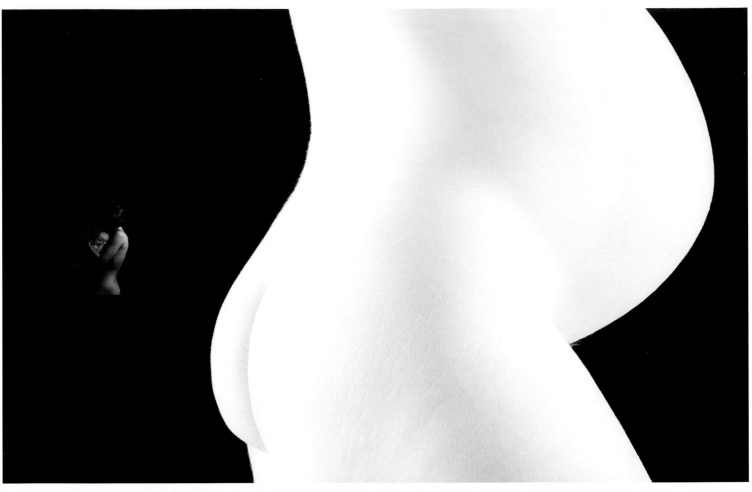
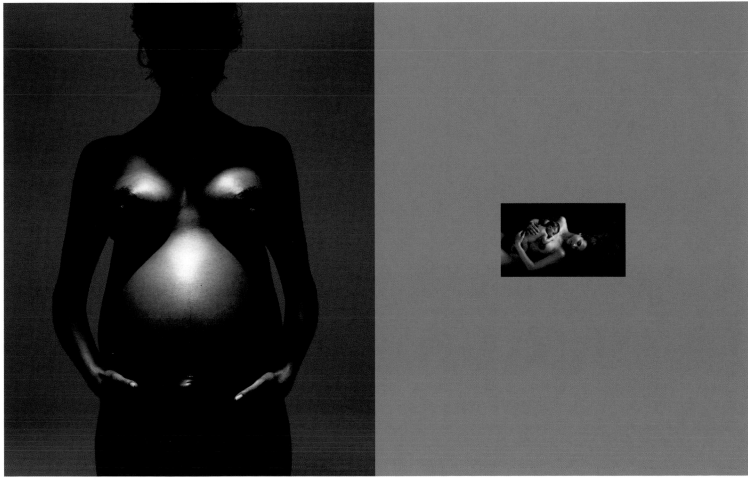

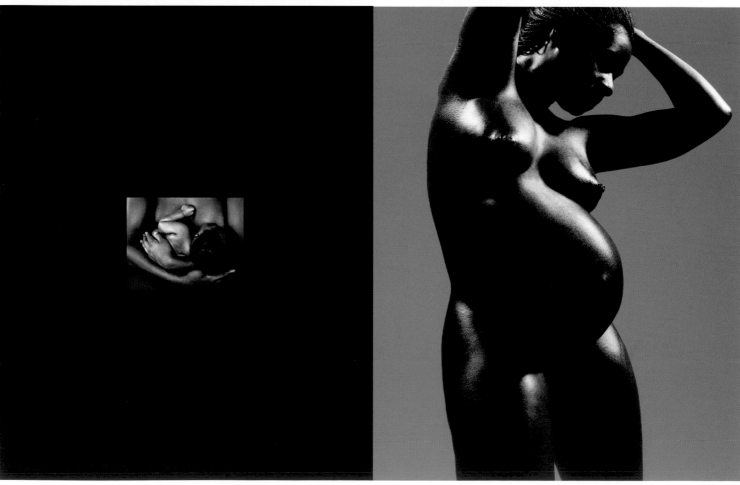

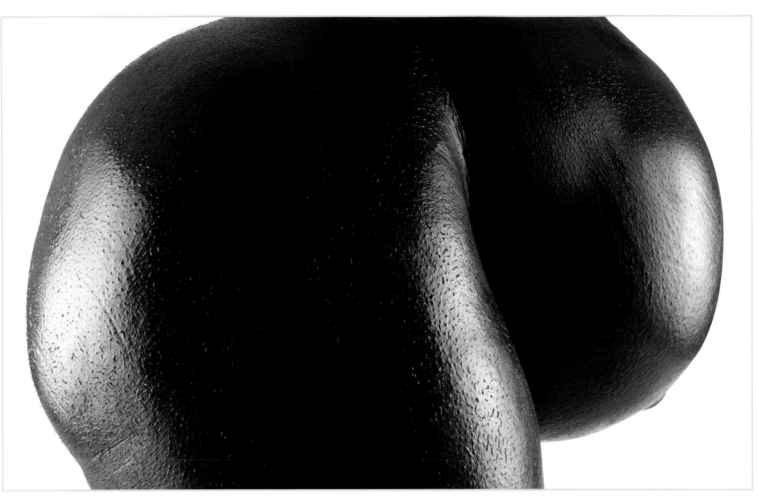

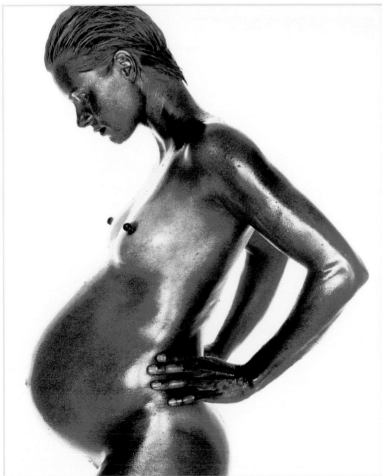

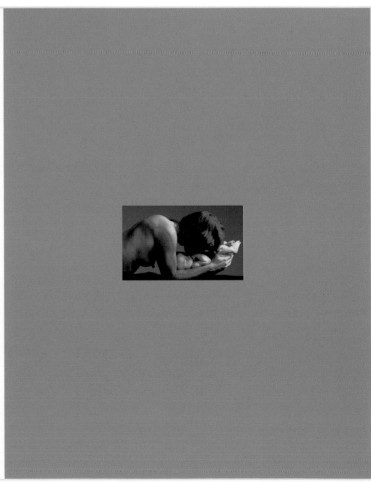

Assignment: Create an architectural monograph for Michael Ryan Architects showcasing the culture of the firm and its process through a selection of marquee projects.

Approach: Before we began the monograph, our first goal was to discover and create the story of the firm. We did this by touring many of the homes designed by the firm, and speaking with former clients who are now close friends. The story we uncovered boiled down to one idea: To create such unique, stunning works of architecture, you must let go of all preconceived notions of what you think you know, and allow for the wonderfully unexpected to unfold. The book had to convey this truth, as well as embody it, by continuously surprising readers with wonderfully unexpected moments. As a whole, the monograph had to feel unlike any other monograph that came before it.

Results: The client was so enthused with the design that they booked a trip to China so they could be on press for the printing of it. They returned with a sample copy, which started helping them win new business from the very first client meeting in which they were able to show it. The book was also picked up by a publisher and is now available for purchase worldwide.

Designer: Justin LaFontaine | **Design Firm:** 160over90 | **Client:** Michael Ryan Architects

I THINK I MAY BE CRAZY

I want to build another house.

"Contemporary culture places an unfortunate emphasis on "knowing what you want" and, of course, "being smart." Unfortunately this works against the design process."

Contemporary culture places an unfortunate emphasis on "knowing what you want" and, of course, "being smart." Unfortunately this works against the design process.

Many clients bring this to the table, and it can hinder discovery and surprise. It is crucial when designing a home that our clients have an open mind with regard to the process. It's all about letting go.

This goes for the architect as well. We need to act as receivers, open to everything that surrounds the making of a building. For us, openness is the ultimate virtue, just one step above optimism.

I work toward an understanding of the potential that really exists, filtering reality from fantasy, and, alternately, creating fantasy from reality.

It is impossible to conjure a building from knowledge only. You need to let go.

LET GO. ring buoy, vinyl letters. 20 inch diameter
JOE BEGONIA, ARTIST, FRIEND & CLIENT.

Assignment: American Odysseys is an anthology of twenty-two novelists, poets, and short story writers.

Approach: The title for this book is printed on a pencil, which is then inserted into a die-cut in the cover. The pencil was chosen as a symbol of the writer and of the writing process. For many of us, the pencil is the first introduction to creating letters, words, and—later on—sentences. The stories contained within are of a personal nature, and the intimate quality of the pencil seemed to be the perfect complement. The pencil is completely removable.

Designer: Joe Shouldice | **Design Firm:** YesYesYes Design | **Client:** Vilcek Foundation

Assignment: The Advertising and Graphic Design Department at the School of Visual Arts invites an established graphic designer, usually someone who teachers at SVA, to create the Senior Library each year. The Senior Library culls work from the graduating class and is meant as both a gift to the students—something by which they can display their work for future jobs and clients—and as a showcase of all of the talent and work emerging from SVA.

Approach: Louise Fili elegantly packaged the Senior Library like a box of chocolates, using rich chocolatey brown colors and her unique type-treatment. The book comes inside a faux "candy" box. When the box is opened you're presented with a *trompe l'oeil* image of chocolates, which serves as the jacket for the book. This makes a unique metaphor for the abundant array of images the viewer will be presented with inside the Senior Library.

Designers: Louise Fili, John Passafiume, Dana Tanamachi | **Design Firm:** Louise Fili, Ltd. | **Client:** School of Visual Arts

Assignment: California Design, 1930–1965: Living in a Modern Way is the catalogue of the eponymous exhibition organized by the Los Angeles County Museum of Art (LACMA), which was on view between October 1, 2011, and June 2, 2012. It was part of "Pacific Standard Time: Art in L.A. 1945–1980," an initiative where the Getty Foundation funded over sixty exhibitions and programs across Southern California. For this first survey of California mid-century design, LACMA's goal was to have the design of the book reflect the special qualities of the state during this period: openness, transparency, playfulness, and joy. In addition to the overall "look" of the book and its cover, the designer had to place over 350 illustrations as close as possible to where they were discussed in the book's ten essays. If they weren't covered in the essays, he needed to find a place where they could be shown to great advantage, and then provide a lucid and visually engaging system of cross-referencing all the illustrations of objects included in the exhibition against the catalogue's detailed checklist.

Approach: During this period, many designers immigrated to California both from Europe and from other parts of the United States, and their responses to the state's distinctive light, space, and color shaped their work. I knew that I wanted this catalogue to reflect that experience—to be bright and open, with white space where possible and with great color in the type. This was a Golden Age of design in California, so the images in the book were incredible: drawings and photos of the Case Study Houses by pioneering architects such as Charles and Ray Eames and Richard Neutra, film titles by Saul Bass, tableware by Heath Ceramics, and furniture by Van Keppel-Green. I felt a huge responsibility to design a book that complemented the work that was being shown in the exhibition and catalogue. I worked closely with the museum photographer, shooting as many pieces as possible against a white seamless ground with minimum soft shadows, rather than using the darker backgrounds found in many exhibition catalogues. I think this really opened up the pages and gave the book the bright feeling I wanted it to have. Similarly, I chose Gotham as the text and headline font, as it has an airy, very readable feel to it.

Results: The curators and the editor believe the designer brilliantly fulfilled all these goals, and the reception of the book certainly substantiates this. Within weeks after the opening of the exhibition, it became clear to the co-publisher, MIT Press, that the company had not printed nearly enough copies, and the run of 8,700 would be sold out well before the end of the show. A second run of 4,300 copies was ordered, and then a third run of 3,550. MIT is now doing a fourth run of 6,000 copies, bringing the total to date to 22,500. In the world of art book publishing, this is extraordinary. According to the publications department at LACMA, *California Design* is among the most successful books the museum has ever published. The book is currently being translated into Japanese. It is a testament to the book's stunning design that the Japanese publisher pursued this before learning that the exhibition was going to travel to the National Art Center in Tokyo, in March 2013.

Designer: Michael Hodgson | **Design Firm:** Ph.D., A Design Office | **Client:** Los Angeles County Museum of Art (LACMA)

Furniture

Ceramics

Architecture

Graphic Design

Industrial Design

Jewelry

LIVING IN A MODERN WAY

CALIFORNIA DESIGN 1930–1965

Fashion

Metalwork

Textiles

DESIGNED AFTER SAUL BASS

Assignment: When Fraenkel Gallery, one of the world's most respected galleries and publishers of photographic works, wanted to create a more ambitious catalogue in support of their solo exhibition of Katy Grannan, they tapped John McNeil Studio to envision and design a substantial yet powerful solution that would feature their artist in the best possible light. The goal was, in effect, to create a catalogue that felt like and could be sold as an art book unto itself. The collaboration for Grannan's exhibition, BOULEVARD, included photographic portraits along Sunset Boulevard in Los Angeles and the Tenderloin district in San Francisco.

Approach: The 15- x 12-inch catalogue, encased in a slightly opaque sleeve, included about forty portraits from Grannan's series, BOULEVARD. The image sequence varies as the photographs randomly alternate from the right to the left side of the page; illustrating the viewer walking down the boulevard. The book also includes a statement from Grannan and a quote from the Kink's song "Celluloid Heroes."

Results: The catalogue was mentioned in many blogs and art book sites as a top book to buy. The exhibition and the catalogue continued to show in New York City at Salon 94 gallery and at the Los Angeles County Museum of Art in 2012.

Designers: Kim Le Liboux, John McNeil I **Design Firm:** John McNeil Studio I **Client:** Fraenkel Gallery and Katy Grannan

Assignment: The St. Louis Public Library Foundation is an independent nonprofit 501(c)(3) charitable organization. First organized by the Board of Directors of the St. Louis Public Library in 1989, the Foundation was reorganized in 2003 and given the charge to increase private-sector support to benefit the growing needs of the Library. The Foundation asked us to create an invitation for their annual gala that would support their chosen theme of "Texts and the City." Their only other direction was that they did not want a simple *Sex in the City* parody.

Approach: We came up with a clever way to take real literary texts and weave them together into an evocative narrative about a gala under the stars in a faraway sparkling city. Each passage was paired with illustrations handcrafted from bits of found book and advertising ephemera. We designed a custom accordion fold, so readers would feel as if they were turning through the pages of the books quoted in the story, with characters coming to life on the pages.

Results: The client's reaction to the finished product was very enthusiastic, as were the reactions of the many invitees. One response sums it up pretty well:

"I received the invitation you designed for the St. Louis Public Library's 'Texts and the City.' Wow! ... getting the clever invitation was reward enough for my small donation to one of my favorite places. You warmed the English teacher of forty-three years in me. Congratulations to whichever individuals are responsible for the idea, the quotes, the format, the execution—everything about the invitation. I hope you all have as much fun designing material like this as I do receiving it." —Sister Barbara Schlatter

Designer and Illustrator: Mary Rosamond Kunnath | **Art Director:** Katy Fischer | **Design Firm:** TOKY Branding + Design
Creative Director: Eric Thoelke | **Account Manager:** Lauren Crevits | **Client:** St. Louis Public Library Foundation

Once upon a time and A Very good time it was...

A PORTRAIT OF THE ARTIST

James Joyce

JAZZ

Toni Morrison

ROMEO AND JULIET

William Shakespeare

THE WIND IN THE WILLOWS

Kenneth Grahame

COLLECTED POEMS

Langston Hughes

WHERE THE WILD THINGS ARE

Maurice Sendak

A TALE OF TWO CITIES

Charles Dickens

PETER PAN

J. M. Barrie

Assignment: 2011 marked the 20th anniversary of Erica Tanov's signature and perennial design, The Erica Tanov Slip. To commemorate the occasion Tanov, the artist Katy Grannan, and Muriel Maffre, the long-standing principal ballerina for the San Francisco Ballet, collaborated on a series of twenty photographs. In the images, Maffre transforms herself into different characters, donning both wigs and various slips, and is captured mid-movement, simulating a series of falls and physical "slips." The photographs, featured in Erica Tanov Stores in New York and Northern California, are all at once beautiful, delicate, and violent. As part of the project, Tanov worked with John McNeil Studio to create a signed, limited edition folio of the work. The book contains twenty images, carefully reproduced as 13- x 17-inch individual offset lithographs plus a folded, limited-edition poster, featuring original illustrations and gold leaf typography. The folio itself has its own delicate details, with a linen cover and a cotton tie that wraps around a de-bossed leather enclosure.

Approach: John McNeil Studio envisioned a design that works as a precious container or memorial—making the book operate more as binder or folio for the collection of photographs. The color palette and illustration style operate in reference to flesh, stitching, and the slip (both the article of clothing and the physical act of slipping). A cotton ribbon and de-bossed ivory leather button fasten the linen folio closed. The book and enclosed poster feature original gold leaf typography and elaborate illustrations designed by the studio.

Results: 20 Years 20 Slips was featured on several fashion blogs, including Refinery 29. The portfolio was sold in Tanov's stores and distributed to Tanov's loyal clientele as a special gift for their years of appreciation.

Designer: Jacqueline Norheim | **Design Firm:** John McNeil Studio | **Creative Directors:** Kim Le Liboux, John McNeil | **Client:** Erica Tanov

Assignment: Febrü designs and produces high-quality office furniture. The communication materials and the general look and feel of the brand did not satisfy the demand.

Approach: The design relaunch focused on simplicity and timeless elegance:

• Attractive product presentation with emotive pictures and minimal graphic design for the necessary technical information.

• Concentration on the product, concentration on the brand—over all channels.

Results: On the basis of the relaunch and optimized use of all channels, Febrü could gain new customers, such as architects, general contractors, and project planners. Better design opened the door to new and different kinds of target groups.

Designers: Christoph Beier, Silke Nehring, André Nickels, Thomas Fiedler, Christian R. Schulz | **Design Firm:** Febrü | **Client:** Febrü

Assignment: Guilford of Maine, a textile manufacturer servicing the contract furniture industry, was being rebranded.

Approach: Guilford of Maine's products were basic go-to products. We came up with the concept of "The New Black" to encapsulate this sentiment. This lead to a black and white showroom, a video of designers talking about the go-to nature of their products, and a new swatch presentation system targeted to each of their vertical markets.

Results: Guilford of Maine's rebrand and reentry into the market was well received. The showroom won awards and the new swatching system created interest again in the eyes of interior designers.

Designer: Peopledesign | **Design Firm:** Peopledesign | **Client:** True Textiles

100% Office
The right amount of sustainability.
Check.

100% Education
The right amount of durability.
Check.

100% Healthcare
The right amount of cleanability.
Check.

100% Office

100% Education

100% Healthcare

Guilford of Maine

Guilford of Maine

guilfordofmaine.com

5300 Corporate Grove Drive SE
Suite 250
Grand Rapids, MI 49512

616 554 2268 Office
800 554 0200 Sales Service

Guilford of Maine

5300 Corporate Grove Drive SE
Suite 250
Grand Rapids, MI 49512

Assignment: The Contemporary team felt that their brand, as expressed in logo, Web site, collateral, and even building, had "gone gray." It felt, they said, too boring, too quiet, too aloof, when what they wanted was to feel engaged with the public, spirited, bright, and new.

Approach: We realized that the old logo was part of the challenge—a single line of elegantly letter-spaced Univers set without breaks. It's sandblasted into the concrete exterior of the building and windows, so it's going to be an essential part of the museum for decades to come. No rebranding can ever move forward without acknowledging this original logo in some way. We broke that logo into a more readable, more usable stack of words, setting them left and right off of a common vertical axis. We also did research and found that only two other museums of contemporary art went by the CAM abbreviation, and neither was geographically proximate. A new consumer-friendly appellation and logo were soon born, now riding on top of that stack of words. After addressing the identity, we moved onto reimagining the newsletter, posters, mailers, exterior and interior signage, and branded merchandise. We rebuilt their Web site from the ground up with a custom content management system. After the success of the Web site, we followed up by creating the CAM app—a smartphone app that gives users a unique museum experience that evolves, whether you are physically in the museum or elsewhere. One of the first museums to launch a fully customized app in St. Louis, joining a handful of leading museums nationally, CAM continues to be a leader in the museum and art fields.

Results: "The entire team at TOKY did a fantastic job rolling out our rebranding campaign. Whether it was a central communications piece, like our Web site, or something that would appear to be more minor, like our new line of T-shirts, TOKY created a comprehensive strategy and delivered ideas that brought attention to our young institution and helped the public better understand us."
—Paul Ha, CAM Executive Director, 2002–2011.

The site went live on 1/11/11. At its launch the CAM site went from a 20-page to a 163-page site with ten authors who regularly update the content. They now have 25,000 hits per month on a site that currently boasts more than 2,550 images.

Designers: Bruce Burton, Katy Fischer, Liz Mohl, Travis Brown | **Design Firm:** TOKY Branding + Design
Creative Director: Eric Thoelke | **Project Manager:** Meredith Maglinger | **Web Designer:** Jay David | **Producer:** Melissa Allen
Developers: Tyler Craft, Kathy Sprehe | **Client:** Contemporary Art Museum St. Louis

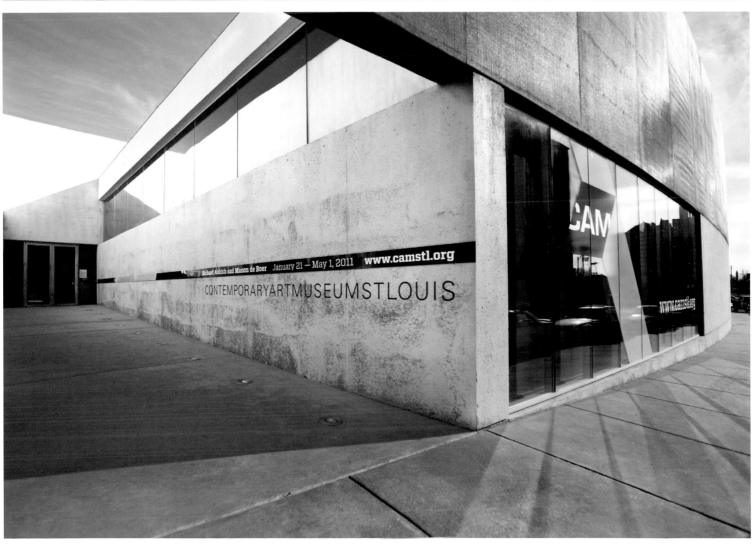

April 2011 / Issue 2

January 2011 / Issue 1

September 2011 / Issue 3

CAM

INSIDE / New Exhibitions / Upcoming Events / The Best Parties in Town

Assignment: Very few brands have touched as many generations around the world as DC Comics has. The brand was determined to continue this legacy. In light of the rapid technological advancements and ever-growing new ways to consume content, DC Comics wanted to expand the reach of the brand and its characters beyond publishing into all new media.

Approach: DC Comics is defined by its characters and stories. It represents a world where opposing forces meet, and where the characters and stories continue to evolve and transform. The new living identity captures this dynamic world. It is ever-changing and adaptive to the superheroes and story lines. The peeling effect reflects the dual identity, the transformative nature, and the depth of personality portrayed by the characters and superheroes. DC is an infrastructure that reveals a world of boundless storytelling—a world where the iconic, the optimistic, and the supernatural coexist.

Results: The new brand and flexibility of execution has unified three different sides of their business that had never previously agreed on the role of brand (publishing, merchandising, and new media). The traffic to dccomics.com doubled after launch. Licensing inquiries increased by 30% just three months after launch.

Designers: Nicolas Aparicio, Martin Bishop, Alice Genaud, Allison Hung, Jill Imani, Martin Kovacovsky, Michael Lin, Junko Maegawa, Kara McCartney, Russ Meyer, Jessica Minn, John Porter, J.P. Sabarots | **Design Firm:** Landor Associates
Client: DC Entertainment (A Time Warner Company)

Assignment: Box Café is located at the entry of a performing arts center (the Aotea Centre) and functions as an information center, ticketing office, and venue. The identity was implemented throughout signage, wayfinding, uniform, collateral, and campaign. Box's location is a strategic one—it is part of a performing arts center located on a popular inner city square—however, there is extensive competition in the area. Box needed a distinctive identity to create an enhanced visual presence that could offer a different experience. It needed to serve as a friendly interface between the public square and the performing arts center. In order to perform well as a multi-functional space, it was essential that careful attention be paid to an internal wayfinding system that could direct customers to which service they required, should it be café service or ticketing.

Approach: Both the name and visual identity needed to simply communicate the offering. The name says what it does—it is a café, a ticket office, a bar, and a lunch destination, as well as a space for private events. The logomark is built from of a series of dots that reference the design vernacular of theater lighting—Vegas, Broadway, or the West End. It also visually references dot matrix printers, commonly found in ticket offices, as well as the configurations of dots produced by punches used to perforate cardboard admission tickets. The mark lends itself to a range of executions and finishes, printed, die cut, embossed, recessed, or floated. This was extended into a broader visual language and series of icons, and a pattern language that communicates the offering in a pictorial sense.

Results: The Aotea Square refurbishment project (of which Box Café was a key element) was awarded the "Public Sector Project of the Year Award" from the Project Management Institute of New Zealand. Box Café has become a social hub that has brought life back into the town square.

Designers: Toby Curnow, Janson Chau | **Design Firm:** Alt Group | **Creative Director:** Dean Poole
Writers: Dean Poole, Ben Corban | **Client:** The Edge

Welcome to BOX.
Please order
from the counter.

Seating provided for BOX patrons only.

Tickets

Assignment: Panera had recently overhauled their company-wide produce delivery system to shorten the time from farm to table. TOKY was tasked to create an emotional story that would connect with their target market, and communicate the idea of freshness, without relying on a dry, fact-based sell.

Approach: The idea of a "Return to Summer" was woven throughout the visual and literal language of all point-of-purchase pieces at Panera bakery cafes nationwide. The concept spoke to the strong sense of memory we all have of warm summer days, but also the return of a favorite—the iconic Strawberry Poppyseed Salad. Beyond that, customers are reminded to return to Panera, to try a new item among the many custom salad options offered throughout the season.

Results: Deconstructed letterpress-inspired typography spoke to the craft and attention put into all of Panera's menu items, from fresh-baked bread to custom salads. This type was used to emphasize choice words that embodied the celebration—the burst of strawberry flavor, the crunch of fresh lettuce, diving into a cool smoothie—an intense flavor experience, and the energy of summer. The color palette and photo styling was authentic, bright, and sun-kissed.

Designers: Katy Fischer, Geoff Story, Eric Thoelke | **Design Firm:** TOKY Branding + Design
Creative Director: Eric Thoelke | **Writer:** Geoff Story | **Client:** Panera

OUR PROMISE

To use tender
CRISP ROMAINE
and JUICY BERRIES
only in season.

To let our TOMATOES
ripen on the vine,
not in a greenhouse.

To deliver all of this
fresh, DAILY and
MADE to ORDER.

Just like a
SUMMER SALAD
should be.

Assignment: "Taiwan and China visually hold the Chinese Characters Festival together, this is the first time Taiwan has held the event alone." Ken-tsai Lee was asked to design the visual identity for the event.

Approach: The Chinese Characters are composed of eight strokes: I used the eight strokes to compose a Chinese Opera Mask—a typeface to represent a Chinese face. I asked the Chinese opera makeup artist to paint the logo onto the face of a Chinese Opera actor to make the poster.

Designer: Ken-tsai Lee | **Design Firm:** ken-tsai lee design studio/Taiwan TECH | **Client:** The General Association of Chinese Culture, GACC

2011
兩 岸 漢 字 藝 術 節

2011
兩岸漢字
藝術節

主辦單位：中華文化總會、中華藝術研究院

合辦單位：
國立歷史博物館、國立台灣博物館
國立國父紀念館、國立台灣藝術教育館
交通部觀光局日月潭國家風景區管理處
台北市政府、國立臺灣藝術大學
何創時書法藝術基金會、台灣印社
台灣數位藝術科技研究所

贊助單位：
富邦藝術基金會
裕隆汽車製造股份有限公司
財團法人台積電文教基金會
永豐商業銀行股份有限公司
中國信託商業銀行

活動內容：
精彩二百 國寶總動員
展期：2011.9.23～2012.1.05
地點：故宮博物院正館二樓

海峽風華－近現代名家書法展
展期：2011.9.22～2011.10.16
地點：國父紀念館中山國家畫廊
岸梅綻實實驗書畫雙年展、
兩岸篆刻名家展
展期：2011.9.22～2011.10.16
地點：國父紀念館二樓西畫

大陸當代藝術展
展期：2011.9.20～2011.10.5
地點：華山1914文創園區四連棟展廳

傳統vs科技藝術展
展期：2011.9.24～2011.10.5
地點：國父紀念館翠溪藝廊入口及中廊

名家對談：蔣勳vs田青
時間：2011.9.24 14:00
地點：台灣藝術教育館南海劇場

兩岸當代書法學術研討會
時間：2011.9.26 8:30～17:30
地點：台灣藝術大學教研大樓國際會議廳

賞義舞墨名家筆會
時間：2011.9.27 15:00
地點：日月潭向山遊客中心

2011
兩岸漢字
藝術節

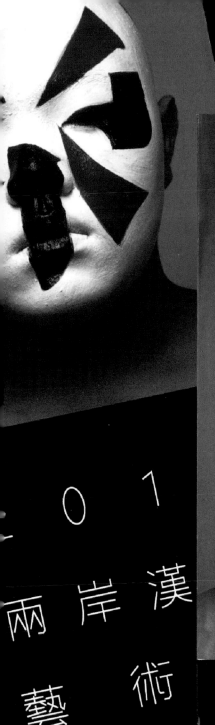

2011

2011

兩 岸 漢 字

藝 術 節

2011.09.23 ～ 2012.01.03

Assignment: These mini posters/leave-behinds were developed for the reintroduction of Interface into the hospitality market. The main function of the pieces was to show interior designers that there are lot of design possibilities for the floor. The pieces were used in a trade show along with other materials.

Approach: We came up with a concept that showcased the product, which is carpet, by using a top-down approach to the photography. The DYF (Design Your Floor) was also part of our concept to help interior designers by encouraging them to use the floor as a design element. We also took the vertical market segments and gave each a visual identity.

Results: We launched this new business segment at a trade show and it was well received. There was a lot of buzz during the show. All the other Interface business units want a similar approach. We are working on phase 2 this year.

Designer: Peopledesign | **Design Firm:** Peopledesign | **Client:** Interface

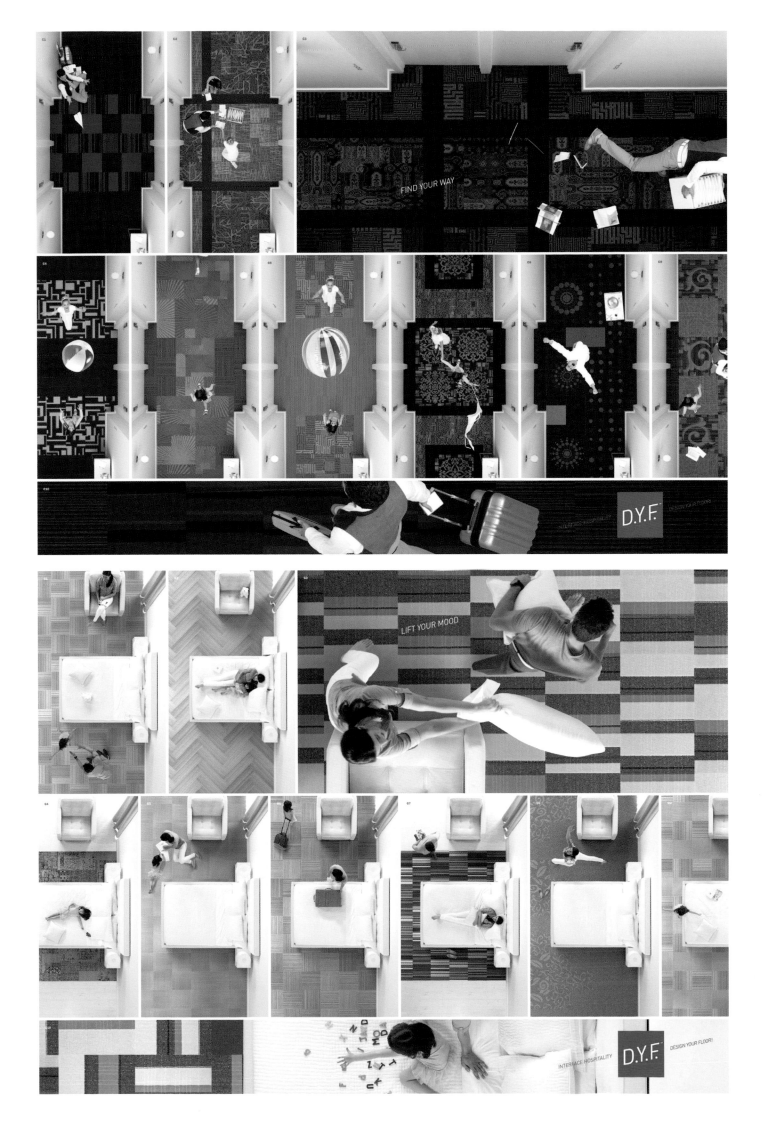

Assignment: To celebrate Sutherland's attendance at the Monaco yacht show and to showcase how wonderfully Sutherland pieces complement the megayacht, we developed a piece that could be used both as a show handout and as a direct mail piece.

Approach: We created a book that very simply and elegantly conveyed the beauty of the furniture. Each piece was considered a work of art, and so we employed some classic chiaroscuro in the photography to add to the drama. In the production, we used an ultra-gloss UV coating to replicate the look and feel of Sutherland's high-gloss yacht finish.

Results: As a direct result of this book, Sutherland has received multiple large yacht orders. That made the client very happy.

Art Director: Tom Nynas | **Design Firm:** David Sutherland, Inc. | **Creative Director:** Tom Nynas
Copywriter: Tom Nynas | **Photographer:** John Wong | **Client:** Sutherland

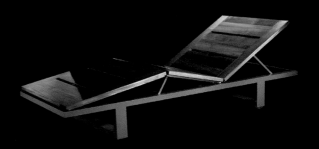

THE SUTHERLAND YACHT FINISH REVEALS TEAK'S
BEAUTIFUL RICH COLOR AND GRAIN LIKE NO OTHER.
IN TRADITION WITH THE WORLD'S GREAT SHIP
BUILDERS, TWELVE COATS OF HIGH-GLOSS MARINE
VARNISH ARE HAND-APPLIED. BETWEEN EVERY
APPLICATION, EACH PIECE IS SANDED AND POLISHED,
AND THE RESULTS ARE SIMPLY BREATHTAKING.

PENINSULA CHAISE | DESIGNED BY TERRY HUNZIKER

POOLSIDE LOUNGE CHAIR | DESIGNED BY JOHN HUTTON

Assignment: This piece is an introduction to Perennials ColorPops collection, a fun and bright collection of fabrics designed for the outdoors, but perfect for anywhere high performance is needed.

Approach: Bright, colorful, and fun describes the new fabric by Perennials, just as they describe candy. So we put the two together into an oversize piece that combines photography and illustration.

Results: The client LOVED the book and apparently so did our market. After this brochure was released, the ColorPops collection sold at a pace three times faster than the previous collection from Perennials.

Art Director: Melissa Tetens | **Design Firm:** David Sutherland, Inc. | **Creative Director:** Tom Nynas
Photographer: Scogin Mayo | **Client:** Perennials

Assignment: Create a product overview book to celebrate the almost 100 year history of a family-owned (third generation) furniture business.

Designers: Michael Vanderbyl, Kellie McCool | **Design Firm:** Vanderbyl Design | **Creative Director:** Michael Vanderbyl | **Client:** A. Rudin

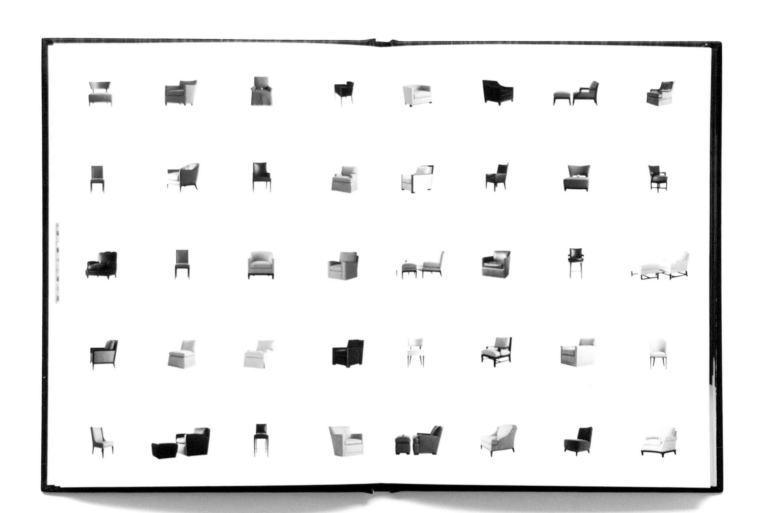

Assignment: We aimed to evolve the previous season's content, with a lookbook that would embody the duality of the Y-3 Spring/Summer 2012 collection.

Approach: The Y-3 Spring/Summer 2012 campaign takes its cue from the vibrant, experimental city of Brasilia. Portraits are collaged with images of archival Brasilia to suggest a delicate balance between the body and the many ways it is contained. The campaign imagery was dispersed throughout the lookbook to contrast with bold, solid-colored backgrounds.

Results: The client was very pleased with the campaign, since the final images embodied the narrative we set out to relay.

Designers: Doug Lloyd, Jason Evans | **Design Firm:** LLOYD&CO | **Client:** Adidas Y-3

This Page: Cupro Tuxedo Pant, W58481. Oriah Shoe, V21190.

Opposite Page: Tech Linen Coat, W57408. Jersey Dress, W57502.
Cupro Tuxedo Pant, W58481. Oriah Shoe, V21190.

This Page: Statement Coat, W42787. Classic Short Sleeve Tee, W38806.
Lux Sweat Pant, W42284. Sly Shoe, V22266

Opposite Page: Pique Cut Blazer, W42798.
Classic Tee, W38806 . Pique Cut Pant, W42867

Assignment: The 2012 Corvette brochure was conceived and developed to highlight the new design of the car and to reconnect it with its racing heritage. The goal was to create a piece that would become a keepsake long after the car purchase. It excited many Corvette fans around the world, and it added layers to the Chevy Runs Deep theme-line.

Approach: We knew it was important to tap into the Corvette's racing heritage. To do that, the entire brochure is written from interviews with the lead Corvette development team. The images were all shot in or around racetracks and the factory. The engineers, drivers, and designers were profiled and photographed, making the entire piece more editorial in both design and copy.

Designers: Keith Anderson, Hunter Hindman, Mike Barton, Rich Conklin, Matt Coonrod
Design Firm: Goodby, Silverstein & Partners | **Client:** Chevrolet

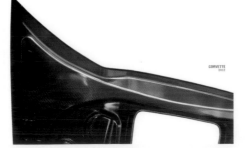

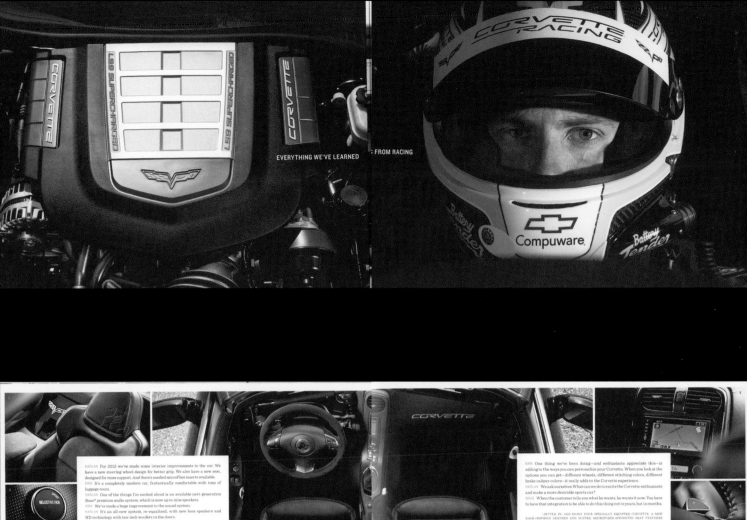

EVERYTHING WE'VE LEARNED ... FROM RACING

HARLAN For 2012 we've made some interior improvements to the car. We have a new steering wheel design for better grip. We also have a new seat, designed for more support. And there's sueded microfiber inserts available.
KIRK It's a completely modern car, fantastically comfortable with tons of luggage room.
HARLAN One of the things I'm excited about is an available next-generation Bose® premium audio system, which is now up to nine speakers.
KIRK We've made a huge improvement to the sound system.
HARLAN It's an all-new system, re-equalized, with new bass speakers and ND technology with ten-inch woofers in the doors.
TOMMY Of course the engine makes the best noise.
TADGE Yes, Corvette has a smart dual-mode exhaust.
TOMMY Smart exhaust?
TADGE It's a vacuum-actuated valve that sits behind the muffler. Back pressure goes down, noise level goes up, and it's all music.
KIRK Dual-mode exhaust is optional on coupe and convertible and on Grand Sport. It's standard on Z06 and ZR1. It gives you six more horsepower!
HARLAN Yep, the dual-mode exhaust actually gives you horsepower, gives you torque. So it has some real functional benefit. But it's almost like the Magnetic Selective Ride Control™ where it creates a car with a dual personality. As a daily driver, when you don't have your foot in too much, it gives you a nice burble in the background. But once you get on it and the tach swings past 3000, those valves open up and it sounds like it's turned into the race car.

KIRK One thing we've been doing—and enthusiasts appreciate this—is adding to the ways you can personalize your Corvette. When you look at the options you can get—different wheels, different stitching colors, different brake caliper colors—it really adds to the Corvette experience.
HARLAN We ask ourselves: What can we do to excite the Corvette enthusiasts and make a more desirable sports car?
DOUG When the customer tells you what he wants, he wants it now. You have to have that integration to be able to do this thing not in years, but in months.

/ SETTLE IN, AND ENJOY YOUR SPECIALLY EQUIPPED CORVETTE. A NEW RACE-INSPIRED LEATHER AND SUEDED MICROFIBER-APPOINTED SEAT FEATURES SUPPORTIVE BOLSTERS TO KEEP YOU COMFORTABLY PLANTED / DIAL IN PRECISE DAMPING CHARACTERISTICS FOR YOUR DRIVING STYLE AND ROAD CONDITIONS, THANKS TO THE MAGNETIC SELECTIVE RIDE CONTROL / A NEW NINE-SPEAKER BOSE® PREMIUM AUDIO SYSTEM WITH 4 TWELVE-MONTH SUBSCRIPTION OR SIRIUSXM SATELLITE RADIO PRODUCES SOUND AS POWERFUL AND REFINED AS THE CAR / WHY DO RACERS LOVE SUEDED MICROFIBER ACCENTS? THEY ARE EASY TO GRIP SOFT, NOT SLICK OR STICKY / NAVIGATE WITH EASE USING A NAV RADIO EQUIPPED WITH ONSTAR® DIRECTIONS & CONNECTIONS™ STANDARD FOR SIX MONTHS. BLUETOOTH® HANDS-FREE CALLING FOR SELECT PHONES KEEPS YOUR HANDS ON THE WHEEL / GEAR UP USING RACING-INSPIRED STEERING WHEEL-MOUNTED PADDLE SHIFTERS / A HEAD-UP DISPLAY PROJECTS CRITICAL INFO ONTO YOUR WINDSHIELD ALLOWING YOU TO KEEP LOOKING AHEAD / GET A GRIP—THE CORVETTE DRIVER'S GRIP PUTS MORE POWER AND CONTROL IN YOUR HANDS.

CHEVROLET CENTENNIAL EDITION GRAND SPORT CONVERTIBLE 412   CARBON FLASH METALLIC

GRAND SPORT COUPE   CARLISLE BLUE METALLIC   AVAILABLE GRAND SPORT HERITAGE PACKAGE   AVAILABLE GRAY BRAKE CALIPERS   AVAILABLE COMPETITION GRAY WHEELS

GRAND SPORT CONVERTIBLE   INFERNO ORANGE METALLIC (EXTRA-COST COLOR)   AVAILABLE SILVER CALIPERS   AVAILABLE CHROME WHEELS

Assignment: This diary was based on the concept of past and future notes. Using a small case with two drawers we separate past from future, switching the small sheets from one drawer to the other, keeping the past as a well-guarded memory.

Approach: We always try to go as far as possible with the concepts we want to illustrate. In this case, the sequence of days associated with a normal diary lead us to this separation of two points in time, past and future, memory and possibility.

Designer: Eduardo Aires | **Design Firm:** White Studio | **Client:** Bitri

Assignment: This piece is an introduction to Sutherland's Mariner collection of luxury outdoor furniture.

Approach: We considered several clever approaches to this book, including shooting the entire book underwater, but when it came right down to it, the beauty of the stainless steel furniture sold itself. So *that* is what we photographed—simple, pure, elegant. In the printing of the brochure, we incorporated a liquid foil to make the metal in the photos shine like real stainless steel. The nickel grommet binding also reflected the construction and materials of the furniture itself.

Results: The results for this introductory brochure are interesting, and they are still coming in. At the initial mailing of the book, Sutherland saw a 20% increase in Web traffic, which is a pretty good sign for things to come.

Design Firm: David Sutherland, Inc. | **Art Directors:** Alicia Christman, Tom Nynas | **Creative Director:** Tom Nynas
Photographers: John Wong, Scogin Mayo | **Client:** Sutherland

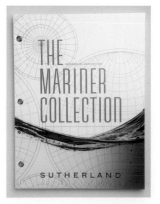

35004 Lounge Chair

35002 Dining Side Chair

35150 Elliptical Coffee Table

Assignment: The daughter of a dressmaker, Lida Baday designs and produces meticulously detailed, beautiful clothing that captures the essence of thoughtful, discerning, and modern women. Lida Baday's collections are sold in luxury boutiques and retailers around the world, including Saks Fifth Avenue.

Approach: Over its fifteen-year relationship with the fashion designer, Concrete has developed the visual language of the brand. The creation of sensual, timeless photography captures the brand's signature style. Luxurious paper and understated detailing combine to showcase the collection in each seasonal campaign.

Designers: Melatan Riden, Leticia Luna | **Design Firm:** Concrete Design Communications
Creative Directors: Diti Katona, John Pylypczak | **Client:** Lida Baday

Fall Winter 2011

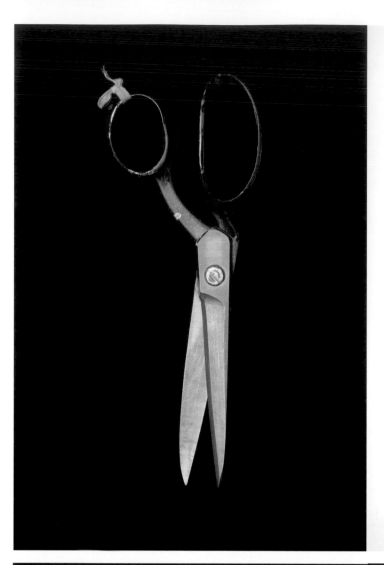

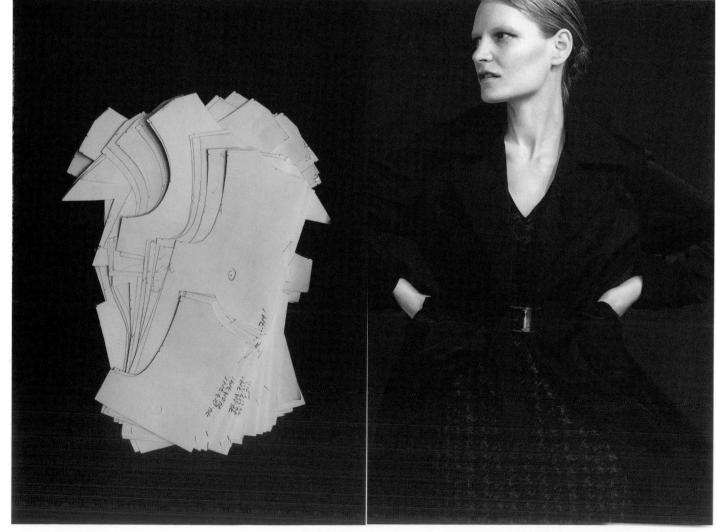

Assignment: The School of Visual Arts Undergraduate Catalog is created each year to show what the School of Visual Arts is and what it offers to potential undergraduate students. The client is the admissions department of the School of Visual Arts and the audience is potential undergrads and their parents.

Approach: The Undergraduate Catalog is an impressively sized catalog—over 600 pages that cover everything a potential student will need to know. The usual information is covered, such as tuition, costs, program descriptions, etc., but what sets this catalog apart is the overwhelming amount of student art in it. There are nearly 500 images in the catalog that illustrate—*prove*—what SVA has to offer. The sheer volume of work is allowable, because we used a small trim size for the book and a very lightweight paper. This also makes the catalog affordable to mail. In addition, we incorporated 3D barcodes into the cover design and throughout the book, to get students to go to SVA's newly designed Web site for more information.

Designers: Michael J. Walsh, E. Patrick Tobin | **Design Firm:** Visual Arts Press, Ltd. | **Client:** School of Visual Arts

Assignment: Arnaud Maggs is an internationally acclaimed Canadian photographer. "Identification" is a survey exhibition that follows the artist's work over the last four decades. The catalogue accompanies an exhibition of his work on display at the National Gallery of Canada.

Approach: When designing this catalogue, we were very much aware of the fact that the design had to be simple, bold, and direct, and not overpower Arnaud's work.

Results: Arnaud had a very successful graphic design and commercial photography career, but at forty-seven he decided to become an artist. It was an honr to work with someone whom we admire so much and who has such a sensitivity and appreciation for design.

Designers: Clea Forkert, Fidel Pena, Claire Dawson | **Design Firm:** Underline Studio | **Client:** National Gallery of Canada

ARNAUD MAGGS: PORTRAIT OF A WORKING ARTIST

Josée Drouin-Brisebois

The photograph is always more than an image: it is the site of a gap, a sublime breach between the sensible and the intelligible, between copy and reality, between a memory and a hope.
GIORGIO AGAMBEN

In 1973, following successful careers as a graphic designer and fashion photographer, Arnaud Maggs, who was 47 at the time, decided to abandon his commercial ventures to become an artist. Embracing his own unique way of seeing the world, Maggs wanted to share his observations with a broader, more diversified audience. In his early works from 1976 through the 1980s he combined an interest in systems of classification and ordering with investigations of human physiognomy. In 64 *Portrait Studies* (1976–78) he organized black-and-white frontal and profile portraits of friends, colleagues and new acquaintances in a monumental grid. Maggs also made a number of photographic works of twins and of fathers and sons, which explore the similarities and differences between close family members.

During a trip to Germany in 1980 Maggs realized some of his most ambitious works: *Kunstakademie* and his portraits of Joseph Beuys. The

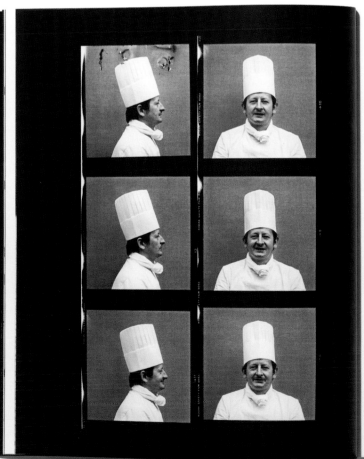

CONTENTS/SOMMAIRE

Approach: Davide Cenci has stood for the best of fashion since 1926. Our catalogue/magazine/travel diary is about a journey through the culture and style of some of the most fascinating regions of the world—told through photographs and copy. All are designed to be the framework in introducing each new Davide Cenci's men's and women's collections, while maintaining the corporate signature's sixty-fifty of the logo in the line of the horizon of every picture. For those hungry for more, we always include a delicious recipe in every new edition.

Designers: Andrea Castelletti, Alberto Baccari | **Design Firm:** TW2 | **Client:** Davide Cenci

16.1 **NYLON MICROFIBER BLAZER**
waterproof
$ 825

17.1 **NYLON MICROFIBER RAINCOAT**
waterproof
$ 795

Royal Pavilion,
Brighton and Hove, East Sussex.

34.1 **SUEDE COAT**
unlined with upholstery closure
$ 1500

34.2 **ELASTICIZED COTTON TROUSERS**
side entry zipper
$ 425

34.3 **PRINTED BLOUSE**
100% silk
$ 375

34.4 **ORDANI HANDBAG**
$ 775

35.1 **BRUNELLO CUCINELLI CARDIGAN**
$ 825

35.2 **CHROME OVER BLOUSE**
100% silk crepe
$ 695

35.3 **KNITTED HANDBAG**
$ 995

Assignment: For Sotheby's Hong Kong Opening Exhibition, the three requirements were:

1) that all collateral for this event had to be bilingual in English and traditional Chinese,

2) look expensive, and

3) illustrate work from the exhibition.

The dot motif was used throughout and was part of the typographic lock-up, which created a strong visual identity that was carried across various marketing and exhibition collateral. The elaborate production specs for the invitation included black type pigment stamped onto a red Plike stock, the logo and date foil-stamped in silver, silver foil edging on the sides, and Kromekote duplexed on the back with white pigment stamped first, then a 4/C process of Kusama's Tulip on top.

Approach: The creative direction we landed on is called Dots Obsession, which plays off of the idea of eternity and the infinite space in the universe that the dots create. This is a motif that is prevalent in Yayoi Kusama's work. She's been called the "Princess of Polka Dots," and indeed, over the course of her astounding sixty-year career, Kusama has blanketed canvases and soft sculptures with them; she's splashed them floor-to-ceiling in her celebrated installations; she's polka-dotted tree trunks (notably, at the 2006 Singapore Biennale); and, during her legendary performance pieces, she's even dotted people. During the approval process, we had to get the artist's sign-off on our layouts. Kusama literally art-directed where and how each dot should be placed, both on the cover and throughout the catalogue. This was accomplished by having her sketch over the layouts, to reposition our dots, and indicating which of those needed to be larger or smaller.

Designers: Tirso Montan, Christina Freyss, Sandra Burch | **Design Firm:** Sotheby's | **Client:** Sotheby's Private Sales

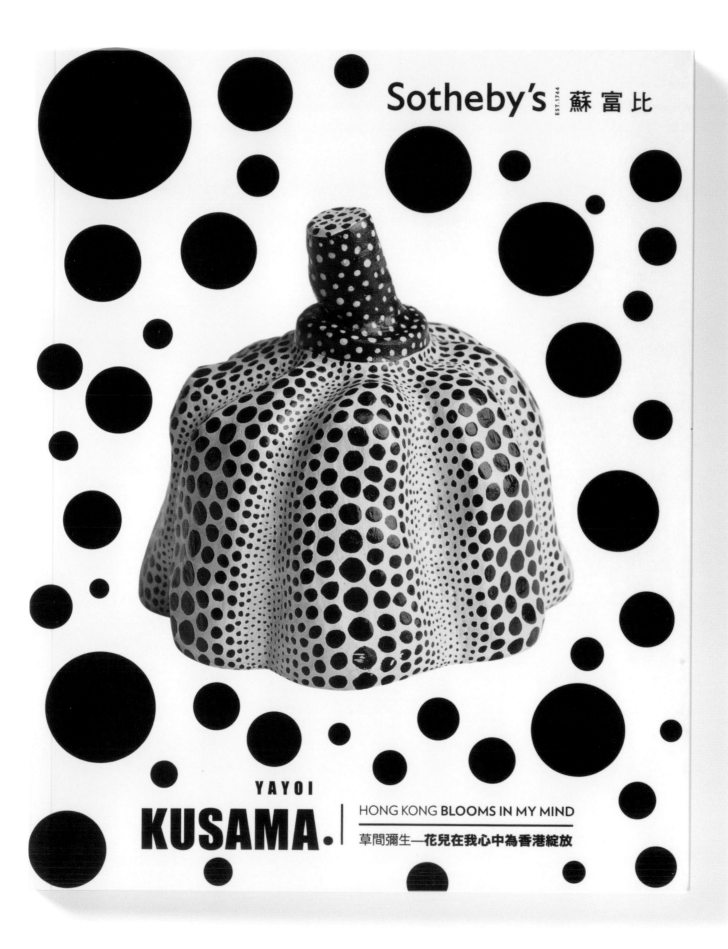

Sotheby's 蘇富比 EST.1744

YAYOI
KUSAMA.

HONG KONG BLOOMS IN MY MIND
草間彌生—花兒在我心中為香港綻放

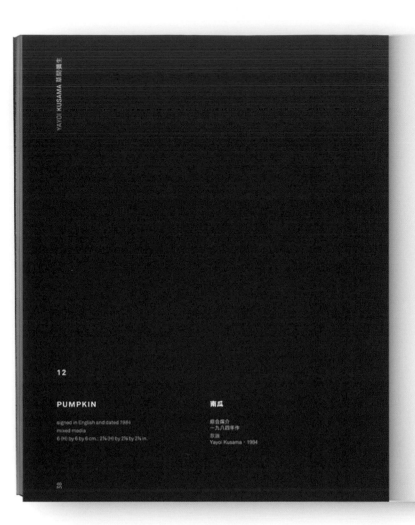

YAYOI KUSAMA 草間彌生

12

PUMPKIN

signed in English and dated 1984
mixed media
6 (H) by 6 by 6 cm.; 2⅜ (H) by 2⅜ by 2⅜ in.

南瓜

綜合媒介
一九八四年作
款識
Yayoi Kusama · 1984

38

Yayoi Kusama, Dots Obsession : Soul of Pumpkin, mixed media, 2002
Harbour City, Hong Kong

Yayoi Kusama with *Pumpkin*, 2010.
Installation view, AICHI TRIENNALE 2010.

14

PUMPKIN

signed in English and dated *1985*
mixed media
8 (H) by 8 by 8 cm.; 3¼ (H) by 3¼ by 3¼ in.

南瓜

綜合媒介
一九八五年作
款識
Kusama・1985

42

Assignment: Lulu is a musical collaboration between Lou Reed and Metallica, based on Frank Wiedekind's *Lulu* plays from the early 1900s. Turner Duckworth was asked to create packaging that reflected the plays and subsequent music in a distinct style that is not normally associated with either iconic artist.

Approach: In the *Lulu* plays, the main character is objectified by men in a brutal tale of sex, deception, and murder. The packaging design reflected this delicate balance between humanity and soullessness by melding the female form with that of a period-appropriate mannequin found in the Museum der Dinge in Berlin.

Designer: David Turner | **Design Firm:** Turner Duckworth Design: London & San Francisco
Creative Directors: David Turner, Bruce Duckworth, Sarah Moffat | **Client:** Lou Reed and Metallica

LULU

LOU REED & METALLICA
LYRICS LOU REED

Assignment: The assignment was to craft a memorable identity that was distinctive from the thousands of would-be solo stars in the UK, and to reflect Avert's musical style with honesty and integrity.

Approach: The process started with an in-depth conversation with the client and artist in order to fully understand who Avert is and the style of music that he is so passionate about playing. Inspiration was taken from photography and well-crafted marks of the last fifty years, using these to create an authentic, organic style that would genuinely reflect Avert and his music.

Results: The repositioning was successful in expressing the folk music side that the client had always wanted to portray, while avoiding the generic look and feel of so many other artists in today's marketplace.

Designers: Marksteen Adamson, Scott McGuffie, Leanne Thomas, Chris Greenwood
Design Firm: ArthurSteenHorneAdamson | **Client:** Lee Martin

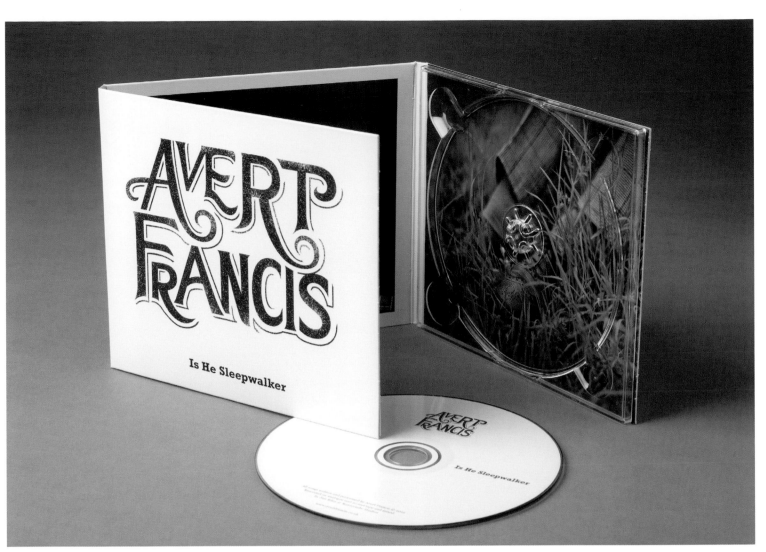
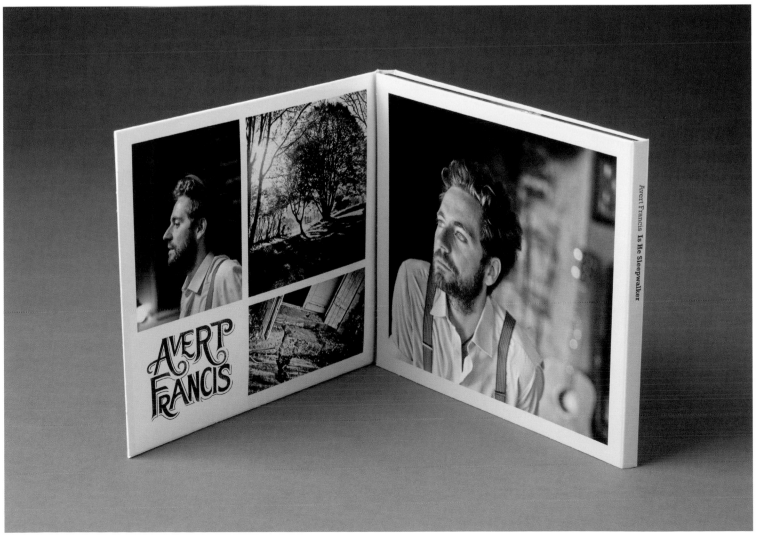

Assignment: These spreads are a collection of stories that were in *AS IF Magazine*'s premier issue.

Approach: IF Studio's approach to the design of the magazine was to be completely non-formulaic and design each image and graphic to relate only to the specific story's editorial content. Overall, we wanted to bring the design of the magazine back to an era when art wasn't designed digitally on computer and was more "handcrafted."

Results: Young to old, everyone who was given the magazine regarded it more like a piece of artwork and coffee-table book, rather than a magazine that you read once and throw away.

Designers: Toshiaki Ide, Hisa Ide | **Design Firm:** IF Studio | **Photographer:** Tatijana Shoan | **Client:** AS IF Magazine
Editor in Chief: Tatijana Shoan

B LACK S WAN

Black Long Gown
with Full Circle
Skirt in Silk Gazar

PHOTOGRAPHY BY TATIJANA SHOAN
ALL DESIGNS BY PETER HIDALGO
STYLING BY JENESSEE UTLEY
HAIR BY SHINYA NAKAGAWA
MAKEUP BY ASIF ZAIDI
MODEL ELY FROM DIRECT MODELS NEW YORK

8

INKED COUTURE AKA TATTOO: GESSO,
ACRYLIC AND INK PAINTED ON
PHOTOGRAPH/PHOTOSHOP

DOTS: INK, AND GOUACHE ON PHOTOGRAPH

MUSE: MIXED MEDIA;
INK, SILVER MARKER ON
PHOTOGRAPH/
MONO-PRINT/PHOTOSHOP

Michelle Violy Harper is known for her singular expression of fashion. Never one to follow trends, she embraces the essence of couture—its lines, movements and statements. She engages in a dialogue with fashion, challenging preconceived notions of what to wear and what not to wear. Her style comes from within, a unique mixture of childhood influences, passion and history. Photographed in the original Tiffany's & Co. landmark building in the midst of a renovation, now named 15 Union Square West, the history and grand interiors acted as a stage for Harper's performance. AS IF Magazine asked Harper to be our muse as we journey through her fashion fantasies eloquently expressed by esteemed fashion illustrator Bil Donovan's brush.

DOPPELGANGER: ALUMINUM
PAINT, ACRYLIC AND BLACK GLASS
ON PHOTOGRAPH/PHOTOSHOP

PHOTOGRAPHY AND INTERVIEW BY TATIJANA SHOAN

INTRODUCTION BY CORY SILVERBERG

MADAME ✕ NINA HARTLEY

90

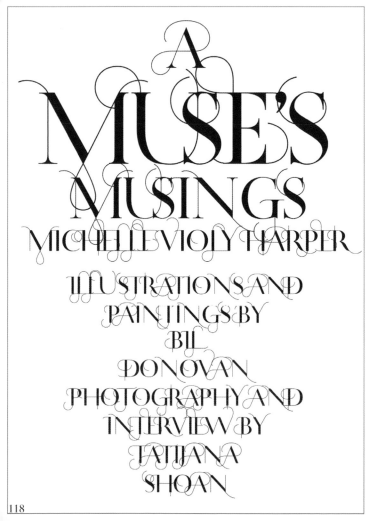

A MUSE'S MUSINGS

MICHELLE VIOLY HARPER

ILLUSTRATIONS AND PAINTINGS BY BIL DONOVAN

PHOTOGRAPHY AND INTERVIEW BY TATIJANA SHOAN

118

HAIR/HEAD PIECE CREATIONS BY SHINYA NAKAGAWA FOR KERASTASE

HAIR ASSISTANT: TY SHEARN

HAIR COLOR: NOELLE CHEN FOR KERASTASE

MAKE-UP BY ASIF ZAIDI

CAGED: CUT PHOTOGRAPH

Assignment: Prefix Photo is a magazine that presents contemporary Canadian photography in an international context. Characterized by innovative design and outstanding production values, it features photography portfolios and critical essays.

Approach: Our design of *Prefix Photo* includes careful consideration of each individual portfolio and essay. We are involved in the entire creative process, from the artists' submission review to final art.

Results: Our seven-year working relationship with *Prefix Photo* allows us to work very collaboratively with them to fully understand their needs and desires.

Designers: Emily Tu, Fidel Pena, Claire Dawson, Scott McLeod | **Design Firm:** Underline Studio | **Client:** Prefix Institute of Contemporary Art

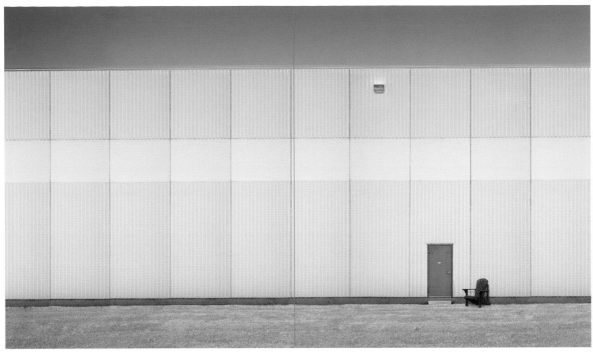

Sudbury vu par...

by Kenneth Hayes

Sudbury's Image

Assignment: Sam Brown was sent home from Afghanistan severely burned. Through immersing himself in a new and experimental virtual-reality therapy, he was able to cope with the horrific pain of his injuries. The recently extinguished but still smoldering headline type says that his once throbbing pain has now been quelled.

Designer: Benjamin Bours | **Design Firm:** GQ Magazine | **Client:** GQ Magazine

Assignment: GQ sent a correspondent to chronicle the adventures of several "real life superheroes"—otherwise unremarkable citizens donning masks and capes in the name of justice. We looked to old superhero comics to inform the layout and treatment of the headline.

Designer: Benjamin Bours | **Design Firm:** GQ Magazine | **Client:** GQ Magazine

BURN ING MAN

On his first tour of duty in Afghanistan, **SAM BROWN** was set on fire by an improvised explosive device. He survived, only to find himself, like thousands of other vets, doomed to a post-traumatic life of unbearable pain. Even hallucinogen-grade drugs offered little relief, and little hope.

Then his doctors told him about an experimental treatment, a painkilling video game supposedly more effective than morphine. If successful, it would deliver Brown from his living hell into a strange new world—a digital winter wonderland
by **JAY KIRK**

Photographs by **ETHAN LEVITAS**

IT'S A BIRD! IT'S A PLANE!

IT'S...

SOME DUDE ?!

THEY ARE ORDINARY MEN IN EXTRAORDINARY COSTUMES, AND THEY HAVE RISEN FROM THE ASHES OF OUR TROUBLED REPUBLIC TO ENSURE THE SAFETY OF THEIR FELLOW CITIZENS. JON RONSON GOES ON PATROL WITH **URBAN AVENGER, MR. XTREME, PITCH BLACK, KNIGHT OWL, GHOST,** AND THE BADDEST-ASS "REAL-LIFE SUPERHERO" OF THEM ALL, PHOENIX JONES

PHOTOGRAPHS BY **PETER YANG**

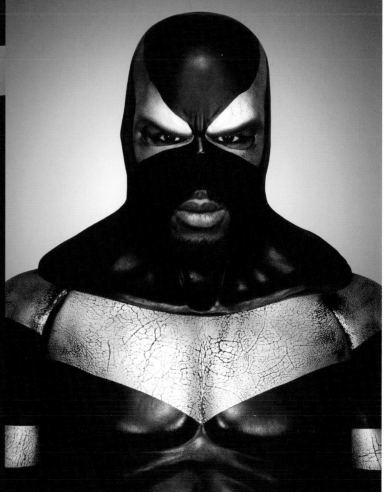

Assignment: This service piece focuses on teaching readers the new rules of wine. We corrected words in the headline to emphasize the transition from age-old wine misconceptions to new wine knowledge.

Designer: Thomas Alberty | **Design Firm:** GQ Magazine | **Client:** GQ Magazine

Assignment: The chaotic cloak of tattoos that completely cover rapper Rick Ross's shirtless body was all the inspiration needed for this story about being a boss. We pieced together found vintage letterforms and frames to create a decorative poster to mirror his massive adorned frame.

Designer: André Jointe | **Design Firm:** GQ Magazine | **Client:** GQ Magazine

"I'M NOT DRINKING ANY F#%*ING ~~MERLOT, PRICEY~~ ~~CABERNET, OAKY CHARDONNAY~~ BORING VINO!"

You chill your whites but not your reds, pair your fancy bottles with fancy food, and skip right past the pink champagne. **GUESS WHAT: You're doing wine all wrong.** We talked to the best sommeliers, vintners, and career winos around to rewrite the book on this fermented-grape-juice thing. And we came up with enough great wine to keep your glass half full till 2012 and beyond

📷 **MICHAEL CRICHTON**

The ~~I~~ NEW RULES ~~s~~ of Wine

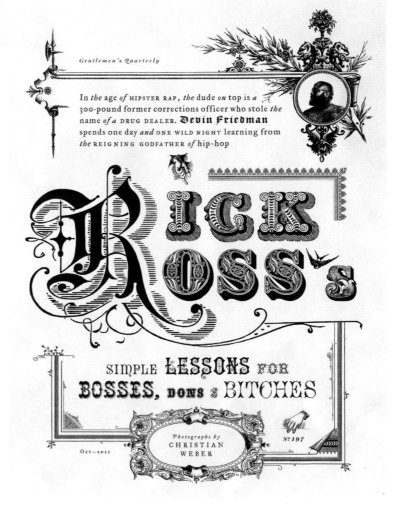

Gentlemen's Quarterly

In *the* age *of* HIPSTER RAP, *the* dude *on* top *is a* 300-pound former corrections officer who stole *the* name *of a* DRUG DEALER. **Devin Friedman** spends one day *and* ONE WILD NIGHT learning from *the* REIGNING GODFATHER *of* hip-hop

RICK ROSS's

SIMPLE **LESSONS** FOR **BOSSES**, DONS & **BITCHES**

Photographs by
CHRISTIAN
WEBER

Oct—2011   № 197

DESTROYING

DETROIT

IN ORDER TO SAVE IT

IT TOOK OVER 300 YEARS TO BUILD THIS CITY. IT'LL TAKE ABOUT FOUR TO KNOCK IT DOWN. **HOWIE KAHN** RIDES SHOTGUN WITH THE MEN WHO ARE DEMOLISHING THE ABANDONED, GODFORSAKEN HOMES OF DETROIT—ALL 70,000 OF THEM—AND PAVING THE WAY FOR ONE LAST SHOT AT THE FUTURE

PHOTOGRAPHS BY TIM HETHERINGTON

135 GQ 5-11

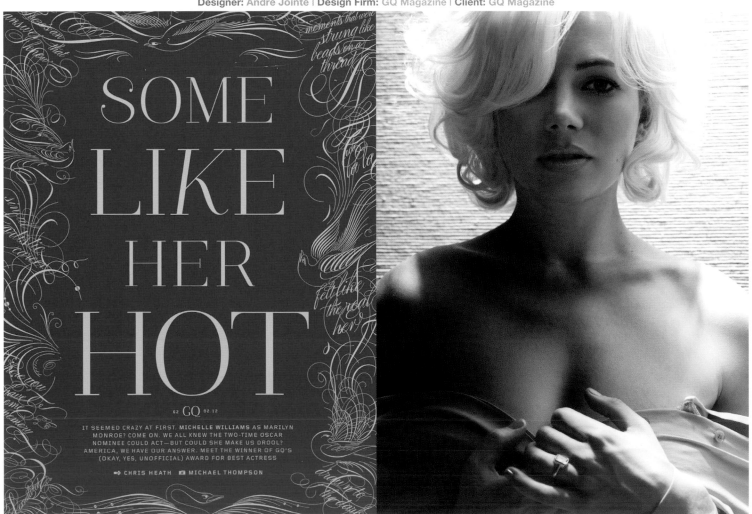

SOME LIKE HER HOT

62 GQ 02 12

IT SEEMED CRAZY AT FIRST. MICHELLE WILLIAMS AS MARILYN MONROE? COME ON. WE ALL KNEW THE TWO-TIME OSCAR NOMINEE COULD ACT—BUT COULD SHE MAKE US DROOL? AMERICA, WE HAVE OUR ANSWER. MEET THE WINNER OF GQ'S (OKAY, YES, UNOFFICIAL) AWARD FOR BEST ACTRESS

➡ CHRIS HEATH ▢ MICHAEL THOMPSON

Jerry-atrics!

He's the original lord

OF LOWBROW,

the king
of the pratfall,
the last
surviving
link to the
bedrock of

burlesque,

slapstick.

—vaudeville,

AMERICAN COMEDY

SURE,
HE'S ANCIENT (85!)

AMY WALLACE

but he's juggling
half a dozen new
projects and still found
time to sit down with

for an eleven-hour

INTERVIEW

call it the

Jerry
Lewis
Marathon

that
covered, well,
just about
everything
that's
ever been
funny

Robert
Maxwell

AUG 2011

118

THE GOOD SEED

60

217

11/9/0

HOW FAR WOULD YOU GO TO HELP YOUR SON
FULFILL HIS DREAM OF HAVING A CHILD?
WHAT IF THAT SON FELL INTO A COMA,
FROM WHICH YOU KNOW HE'LL NEVER
EMERGE? WOULD YOU REACH INSIDE HIM

TO EXTRACT AND PRESERVE HIS LEGACY?
IF YOU WERE NIK EVANS'S MOTHER, YOU
WOULD—AND YOU'D START A PATERNITY
FIGHT THE WORLD HAS NEVER SEEN
▶ DAN P. LEE

Assignment: Over thirty Rock'n'Roll legends were photographed by Mark Seliger for this portfolio. We chose a classical didone typeface to reflect the timelessness of the subjects and cast the shadow of the "I" in the opposite direction from the rest of the characters to reflect each musician's singularity.

Designer: Thomas Alberty | **Design Firm:** GQ Magazine | **Client:** GQ Magazine

Assignment: GQ's food critic, Alan Richman, eats his way through San Francisco, California, declaring it the most exciting and innovative city in American food right now. We designed custom letterforms using graphic shapes and two colors that overlap each other to emphasize the boldness of the food being created by each chef featured in the story.

Designer: André Jointe | **Design Firm:** GQ Magazine | **Client:** GQ Magazine

The

SUR VIV ORS

DRUGS. BOOZE. MONEY. FAME. They have derailed or ended the careers of many of the most inspired musicians. Of those who keep going, only a few evolve—even flourish—long enough for us to still be listening ten, twenty, even fifty years later. The forty-six artists here are the ones about whom you'll never say, "I only like their early work." These are the legends and legends-in-the-making who refuse to die, quit, back down, or shut up

Portfolio by **Mark SELIGER**

I ♥ SF

How did it happen that New York's food scene suddenly became a little...predictable and the one place that's serving up innovation after innovation is ever-p.c. San Francisco and once-grubby but increasingly vibrant Oakland? **Alan Richman** eats his way through the most exciting movement in American dining right now

This page: Carrot-fennel soup with puffed tapioca at Commonwealth.

Opposite page: The black-truffle xiao lung bao (soup dumpling) at Bena.

Assignment: For *Members Magazine*, we wanted to deliver the PROUD brand identity to reflect the company's thought.

Approach: We found the best solution was to use typography to create new looks to communicate the magazine's concept to readers.

Designer: Osamu Misawa | **Design Firm:** omdr design agency | **Client:** Nomura Real Estate Development Co., Ltd.

下に敷いたカーペット「MUNI CARPETS」/MUNI 南青山本店
ジョン・ボッジオ フォー フランク プレート「Marmoseta」/フランス風化加研研
タッセル 豪小「h&d」 カップ 読書の壁掛けオブジェ/シノワブリーワーク ガラス マンダリン
鳥のクッション/ローラ アシュレイ ジャパン ジョン・ボッジオ フォー フランス
水のフラワーベース「Summer Garden」/フランス恵比寿三越店
真んこのオブジェ、アンバーガラス プレート、ゴールドのフレーム/sind

Chinoiserie to Modern times

現代の暮らしにシノワズリーの趣を

文│本間美紀
text by Miki Homma

写真│宮本昭二
photograph by Shoji Miyamoto

スタイリング│中林友紀
styling by Yuki Nakabayashi

ヨーロッパで流行した美術様式、
シノワズリーの世界には、時を越えて
人の心を引き込む魅力があります。
中国の文化が持つ強さを活かしながら、
日本の暮らしにうまくミックスさせる。
そんな配分の妙を、探ります。
バランスの鍵は、「洋」の差し方にありそうです。

フロア畳「TATAMI ST.」/畳・藤・亜/凛品風出店
土と吉田三二「枯割トレイ」/TEORI トレイ上 和宮 ラウロ「ankaa」/ライナー/神戸針発両院
CUIOKA 新取「ボール/セブプレオ」取付外木鉢とリーン濃「Rie 明日セニゾの新作チラップ/池田明子
トート「KIKU」一杯を着き/KIKU レンゴントンメーネード・トレー/CUIOKA ホーツ神と/どシメンジ地流れ
白山陶器 モスカット レター22スタンド 「有」HAKUSAN SHOP 富士山ランプ/フンズ・フィズ トゥールス
フリー スタッドボトル「THE COVER NIPPON」大豆ガラスにこまし、ブンカボーン/ふ
Karin 新宮 ガラスブクト ウェオトコセント ホーキ小トヤスト 竹製承掛け/「SCROLL」/TEORI おしゃれ座五刀/寿和風和店
葉/「THE COVER NIPPON」HASAMI 榎木盆、「ハニムムボット/4」/マリ&ヒロ

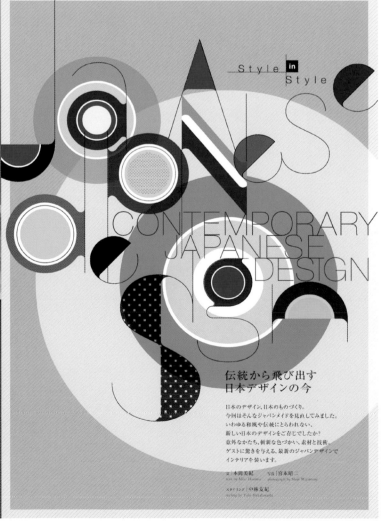

CONTEMPORARY
JAPANESE
DESIGN

伝統から飛び出す
日本デザインの今

日本のデザイン、日本のものづくり。
今回はそんなジャパンメイドを見直してみました。
いわゆる和風や伝統にとらわれない、
新しい日本のデザインをご存じでしたか？
意外なかたち、斬新な色づかい、素材と技術。
ゲストに驚きを与える、最新のジャパンデザインで
インテリアを装います。

文│本間美紀　写真│宮本昭二
text by Miki Homma　photograph by Shoji Miyamoto

スタイリング│中林友紀
styling by Yuki Nakabayashi

Assignment: The design for Luna Textiles, a commercial textiles company, was approached with two challenges in mind. The space had to function as a showroom featuring the company's expanding product line, as well as function as an office for the regional sales manager. The resulting design is an expansive space that has a seamless dual function. A minimalist approach was implemented to create an open environment and provide space for highlighting new product launches. Flexibility in display options is accomplished with a series of wall hooks that presently display custom hatboxes upholstered in Luna fabric. This presents a subtle yet creative illustration of Luna's capabilities. The display is annually updated with new fashion objects. The entry wall displays the Luna Textiles corporate statement in a bold yet subtle way in light grey typography. The statement reads:

"Luna textiles believes in the need for new ideas in all types of design, textile design included. We are inspired by 'good design' of all kinds—interiors, architecture, graphics, and fashion—each field with a unique point of view. Luna believes that excellence in all things comes from discovering your strengths, keeping them in sharp focus, and acting on them to the best of your ability. We do not strive to be the biggest, but simply to be the best source of well-designed, elegant, and refined textiles today and into the future."

Blind-door paneled double-sided cabinets run the width of the showroom behind the display and separate the display area from the conference area with an abundance of storage space to maintain the minimalist aesthetic. Three long display/work tables anchor the symmetrical interior, with three chandelier lights for viewing fabric swatches. These "library" tables allow flexibility of viewing of the product by several individuals at the same time. A conference room at the back divides the space with an area for private meetings or larger gatherings. Blind doors in the conference area conceal all office equipment. Curtains made of Luna textiles provide exterior window light control. The design elements of white laminate walls, black and white striped carpet, custom white tables, and white chandeliers contrasted with Luna Textile's colorful product creates an open, flexible space that gives the illusion of being much larger than its modest 1,650 square feet. The overall effect is one of elegant simplicity.

Designers: Michael Vanderbyl, Peter Fishel, David Hard I **Design Firm:** Vanderbyl Design
Creative Director: Michael Vanderbyl I **Client:** Luna Textiles

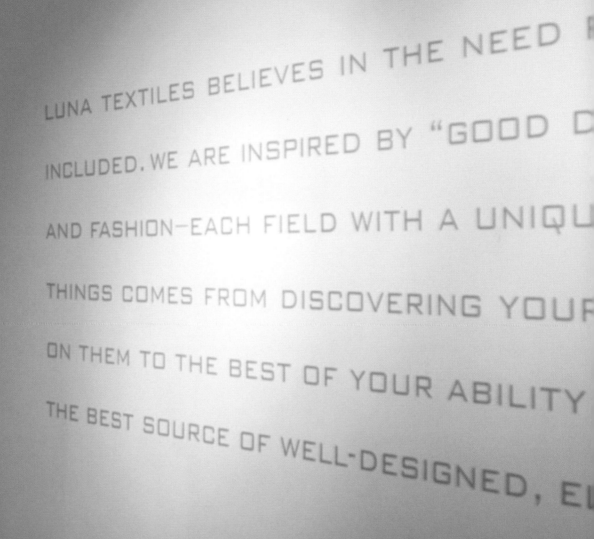

LUNA TEXTILES BELIEVES IN THE NEED
INCLUDED. WE ARE INSPIRED BY "GOOD D
AND FASHION—EACH FIELD WITH A UNIQU
THINGS COMES FROM DISCOVERING YOUR
ON THEM TO THE BEST OF YOUR ABILITY
THE BEST SOURCE OF WELL-DESIGNED, EL

Assignment: Teknion, an international manufacturer of contract office furniture, wanted to give its Atlanta showroom a fresh look that would surprise and delight those who enter the space—and set the stage for its diverse product line. A third mission was to create a facility that would qualify for LEED® Gold. The challenge was to work with an L-shaped site and a cavernous space with soaring ceilings. The solution was to paint it white. Bold color is used with restraint as punctuation. And rather than fight the inherent structural qualities of the buildings, the design team chose to accentuate its verticality.

Within the 7,259-square-foot showroom, white "pleated" walls rise from the floor to the ceiling, lending dimension, texture, and a reflective surface that makes the most of daylight streaming into the showroom from storefront windows along two sides. As light passes through the space and plays over the surfaces, the "color" of the white walls is transformed and intriguing shadows add nuance to a serene yet powerful interior. Floors are raw concrete polished to retain their utilitarian simplicity and provide a contrast to the walls.

Upon entering the showroom, visitors encounter one wall constructed of eucalyptus wood behind the reception, which establishes entry by its placement and contrast to the white-on-white setting within. Walking through the space, one meets strategically placed screens with the same pleated construction as the floor to ceiling walls. The partitions create visual layers and define zones that allow visitors to focus on individual groups of furniture. A left turn reveals an unexpected element as the visitor glimpses a glowing orange wall through a crisp white grid that displays individual chairs like works of art. Beyond making a vivid statement, the orange wall also sets off the showroom's back-of-the-house workspace and equipment.

The Atlanta showroom succeeds both as a statement and as a neutral backdrop that allows the furniture to have more impact than it would in a space where colors of all kinds compete for attention. The design concept is especially effective in making use of Teknion's Altos and Optos architectural wall systems. Here and there, Altos and Optos pierce the faceted white walls, creating small "private offices" with transparent fronts that contribute to the airy look of the Teknion showroom—and to the diffusion of natural light. Pure, clean, and contemporary, the Atlanta showroom offers a bold, yet elegant use of materials and space to show off Teknion's diverse product line.

Results: Teknion's Atlanta showroom has qualified for and has been submitted to receive LEED® Gold Certification.

Designers: Michael Vanderbyl, Peter Fishel, David Hard | **Design Firm:** Vanderbyl Design
Creative Director: Michael Vanderbyl | **Client:** Teknion

Assignment: Delta Air Lines, one of the world's largest carriers, caters to business travelers through its more than fifty Sky Clubs located in airports all over the world. The Sky Clubs have always served as one of the most important touchpoints for communicating Delta's brand experience, and as customers' needs evolved, it was essential for Delta to keep pace. The overall goal of this project was to reimagine and redesign the environment, amenities, and overall experience of Sky Clubs in order to build share and loyalty among its highest value customers. The result: a style and experience that is distinctly Delta and has answered the call of how to travel better through design.

Specific goals of the project included:

- Revitalize the existing Delta Air Lines Crown Room to align with Delta's new brand positioning and identity.
- Create a distinctive club environment that infuses the Delta brand essence and incorporates "Sky" cues for a unique and memorable brand experience.
- Offer amenities and unexpected surprises that engage the premium business traveler.
- Build brand consistency through a flexible framework of shared design principles, core identity components, and secondary elements that can be implemented across multiple locations.
- Enhance overall perceptions of Delta as an airline of choice.

Approach: With Delta's brand positioning, personality, and visual identity as a guide, the team utilized a proprietary Customer Experience Mapping® process to take a broad view of the experience Delta offered and identify ways to enhance it throughout every touchpoint. A multi-faceted team of graphic and industrial designers, architects, strategists, and user-experienced experts looked deep within the brand, its competitive set as well as benchmarks outside of the industry such as luxury hotels and restaurants. All the while, they intensely focused on the needs of the premium business traveler who would be key to embracing the new Sky Club and advocating it to others.

An exciting new experience, design, and set of signature amenities came from the intelligent application of a few core principles rather than rote repetition of design elements. For instance, the concept of "D-location" was developed with the intent of shifting traditional customer experiences and creating differentiation. This included the ability to print a boarding pass at home, watch HBO in flight, view flight information on your mobile, and other elements that today are considered table stakes.

The Sky Club experience also incorporated different zones that embodied the brand essence of "Every Moment Matters." Each zone was filled with amenities tailored to save—or enhance—time for the traveler. Specifically, the team designed places to refresh, play, work, relax, and recharge, mixing communal areas with more private ones.

Finally, in the air and on the ground, sensory cues, including sights, scents, textures, and sounds enhanced the overall experience, making it more engaging, distinctive, and memorable.

Other unique design solutions included:
• The Sky Club Artwork and undulating ceilings inspired by the incredible landscape and destinations encountered in flight from the window seat were further examples of the "D-Location" principle.
• Delta's "Blue Skies Scent" was developed in alignment with the brand essence, evoking freshness, warmth, the color blue, and spaciousness.
• Curated soundtracks of modern sounds created an elegant ambience and energy, while a variety of playlists were tailored to different times of day.
• The core Delta brand identity was brought to life through distinctive materials and finishes, including the use of blue glass, dimensional diamond pattern walls, linear wood veneers, glowing surfaces, and translucent mesh partitions.

The Customer Experience sequence was as follows:
• An entrance that is distinctive and easy to find—welcoming and hospitable with a sense of graciousness.
• A reception area that keeps up with the speed of travel—warm and hospitable with an emphasis on efficiency.
• The heart of the lounge is very much like the home kitchen; guests can socialize or just tune in to a variety of media. Amenities include self-serve beverages, snacks, and entertainment.
• Like being in your own living room; guests can enjoy a movie or other entertainment, or socialize with other guests in a lounge or cafe environment.
• A modern expression of business travel; free wireless access and a choice of work areas, from casual lounge seating to work counters and conference rooms—enhancing guest productivity to make the best use of their time.
• A variety of furnishings to sit back and unwind—a place where guests can read a book or listen to music, either among others or in the privacy of their own comfortable space.
• Bold, distinctive, and thoughtful restrooms—an eyebrow-raising, iconic environment with refreshing amenities.

Designer: Terry Liu | **Design Firm:** Lippincott | **Creative Director:** Connie Birdsall | **Partners:** Fabian Diaz, Adam Stringer
Associate: Joey Rippole | **Client:** Delta Air Lines

Assignment: The Weston Family Learning Centre at The Art Gallery of Ontario heralds the potential of the 21st century art museum as a social hub for community creativity and learning. Through direct and hands-on encounters with art, artists, and the creative process in the studio setting, people from across Toronto and Ontario province experience the power of art to transform how we understand ourselves and our world. More than just a building project, the Weston Family Learning Centre acts as a catalyst for creative inquiry, innovation, imagination, and lifelong learning. It is a project that has established three very distinct capabilities—capabilities that will allow the AGO to extend the range and reach of its education programming to larger and more diverse audiences. These capabilities include:

New Profile:

- a dedicated entrance declaring the AGO's commitment to art education with street-side presence, publicly marking its place at the forefront of Gallery life
- a new presence for art education in the life of the city

New Spaces and Capabilities:

- double the capacity for students through the creation of a new and larger entrance and exit ramp
- students and teachers being welcomed into custom-designed, dedicated spaces for their particular needs—lockers, lunch facilities, and orientation
- custom-designed dedicated spaces for students and teachers, for youth programs and for an artist-in-residence studio, in addition to a visual media lab for digital media art projects
- an ability to reach new and established audiences, particularly students and teachers throughout Ontario, delivered through new technologies and online education programs and resources

New Programs:

- providing access to the Gallery for students and teachers who would not otherwise have the means to participate
- new programs such as the Neighbourhood Access program offering free admission to schools within walking distance of the Gallery
- a public showcase for presenting community art such as the highly successful *In Your Face* exhibition, consisting of 20,000 portraits submitted by people around the world
- an Artist-in-Residence program providing advanced students and artists master classes and instruction, and direct access for the public to practicing artists at work in the studio
- renewed discipline and expansion of research and program evaluation practices to measure the impact of programming

artist in residence stu
education comm
gallery sch
hands-on cer
libr
community gall
seminar roo
thea
youth ce

WESTON FAMILY learning centre

Project Goals:

1. Functional: durable

2. Flexible: maximizing space and program opportunities

3. Accessible: feeling of welcome

4. Integrated: direct connection to the galleries

5. Transparent: inviting visitors behind-the-scenes

Approach: Entro | G+A's approach to a specific task can be called "Classic Avant-garde." It is classic, because our design is timeless and based on values as old as mankind, like harmony, symmetry/asymmetry, and proportion; it is avant-garde, because we don't have a style that we apply to every project; each solution is unique to its specific situation, context, and Zeitgeist. It is also avant-garde because we add an artistic view to a signage project. This art-influenced approach is visible in many of our projects.

In the Weston Family Learning Centre, information was organized and grouped according to importance. As we have seen in other museums, programs are constantly in flux, spaces are reorganized and reassigned to new tasks. We took great care to keep the sign system flexible and expandable, which meant that some information need not even be displayed as a physical sign, but can be available through digital information screens. Also, the sign system was simple and easy to fabricate, yet sophisticated in appeal and innovative in design.

Results: "I just want to say how elegant the design is and, above all, how beautifully visible it is." —AGO Design Studio

Designers: Udo Schliemann, Ian White, Tobias Mikel, Darren Rodenkirchen I **Design Firm:** Entro I G+A I **Client:** The Art Gallery of Ontario

youth
centre

17 18

3 4

67

↖ galler
← semin
artist
washr
elevat

Assignment: After announcing its plans for a $250 million retail redevelopment at the World Financial Center in New York City, Brookfield Properties identified retailers as a new marketing target. At ICSC's RECON conference, Brookfield requested an iconic island space where representatives could showcase their firm's world-class services amid a powerful visual representation of their brand. Logistically, the exhibit needed to provide high-tech meeting rooms, public space, storage space, and a monumental entrance that could be seen from across the exhibit hall. It also needed to be flexible enough to be reconfigured and moved to different locations, and compact enough that it fit within a 40- x 30-foot space.

Approach: The exhibit was inspired by the minimalist, modern design approach taken at Brookfield's New York City headquarters. The design team kept the exhibit's overall material palette simple, using a metallic laminate to mimic metal architectural panels. To warm the cool metallic facade, they used Carrera marble for table and desk tops, and Coach leather fabric for the seating. From a distance, Brookfield's projects were showcased via a series of unified video monitors at the front of the space. Upon closer inspection, this gateway feature was accompanied by casual, comfortable seating for visitors to use while waiting for a meeting room to become available. A glowing glass reception desk identified the Brookfield identity gracefully. Three separate meeting rooms for private conversations exist within the space, each expressing a consistent, high-quality design vernacular—a rarity for trade show exhibits. Television displays are sunken into the wall in an effort not to disrupt the sleek lines of the space. Additionally, overhead lights shine from a canopy above, providing the illusion of a ceiling within the tall convention hall. Amidst all the other show exhibits, the Brookfield booth appeared less as a temporary space and more as a permanent office where real business is accomplished.

Results: The exhibit dominated the showroom floor, making a dramatic statement to passersby about Brookfield and its mission, and introducing the firm boldly to potential retail clients. Visitors remarked on its uniqueness. "You couldn't pass it by without stopping; it was very impressive," was a comment shared repeatedly with Brookfield's exhibit receptionist. Following the success of the exhibit, the design team was asked to replicate the media wall within Brookfield's headquarters as a major element within its repositioning program.

Designers: Jan Lorenc, Stewart Sonderman, Steve McCall, Chung Youl Yoo
Design Firm: Lorenc+Yoo Design & Journey Communications, Inc. | **Client:** Brookfield Office Properties Inc.

Assignment: Omni Apparel is an umbrella business covering six of Australia's best known underwear and hosiery brands: Berlei, Holeproof, Jockey, Razzamatazz, Rio, and Voodoo. The challenge they presented to us was to develop a brandmark that could represent the entire business. Using the common element of the six component brands—the literal thread of the story—to form the "O" for Omni, we developed a simple, fresh design that reflects the dynamic nature of the business and the evolving, vibrant industry they are part of.

Approach: We were asked to find a way to bring Omni's new brand to life inside the company head office. We created a sculpture of the newly designed brandmark. We used the continuous thread of the logo to link the various areas within the building. We then highlighted the different zones in the building by showing how the thread was made up of the various brand names within the business—all of which flowed through to a monumental brand wall in the foyer. We also used the design elements of this wall to define core usage areas—such as the cafeterias or break rooms.

Design Firm: Peel Design | **Creative Directors:** George Margaritis, Rita Palmieri Trsan
Production Manager: Michael Chubb | **Client:** Pacific Brands Underwear Group

Assignment: A cornerstone of IBM's centennial year celebration, THINK was a multimedia exhibition that brought to life the many ways in which people are making the world work better through innovation. It was free to the public, drawing 25,000 plus diverse visitors—from CEOs to school kids—in its month-long run at NYC's Lincoln Center. THINK consisted of three distinct experiences: real-time data visualizations of NYC systems rendered on a 123-foot LED wall; a ten-minute film played in an immersive media field of forty 85-inch plasma screens that then became forty touch-screen interactive modules during the interactive portion of the experience. The purpose of the exhibit was to build constituency around a big idea, one that is core to IBM but much broader than IBM. The exhibit focused on progress—how it happens and how it can be accelerated by technology.

Approach: The exhibit had to be both relevant to scientists and CEOs and fun and engaging for kids. The team worked with a broad range of experts—from researchers building traffic models to biologists studying the rice genome—to ensure that every detail of the exhibit was scientifically accurate. Then the team of designers, filmmakers, architects, developers, and artists translated the science into an emotional and visceral experience utilizing some of the most current technologies. As visitors approached Jaffe Drive, they were drawn to the exhibit by the brightly animated 123-foot LED wall that extended the entire length of the ramp leading to the interior exhibit entrance. Once inside the lobby, visitors were greeted by staff members, could view the show times and get a ticket, and read the introductory text panel before entering the theater. Once inside the theater, visitors were enveloped within the darkened space. Mirrored walls extended the environment into infinity, and subtle lighting dimmed as the film experiences began on the forty plasma screens. Visitors could choose to stay in one place during the film, or wander about to experience the immersive media from different vantage points. When the film ended and the interactive experience began, visitors were once again encouraged to move around and explore the five different touchscreen interactives. THINK was inspired by IBMs 1964 World's Fair Pavilion, which ignited widespread interest in computing and set the stage for the technological revolution. Just as the pavilion demystified the complex scientific concepts of that era, THINK aimed to define today's conversation about technology.

Results: More than 25,000 people came to THINK in its short four-week run. IBM polled visitors as they left the exhibit and found that 88% of adults and 91% of kids said they enjoyed the experience a lot, and more than 70% of adults said they felt inspired to think of ways we can make the world a better place in which to live. The press and social media coverage of the exhibit experience was overwhelmingly positive, with everyone from a *New York Times* art critic to retirees and high school kids sharing information about the exhibit and telling the people in their networks to visit. Coverage included features by the *New York Time*s, ABC News, *Scientific American*, Engadget, the *Huffington Post,* Fast Company, and many other outlets.

Design Firm: Ralph Appelbaum Associates, Inc., SYPartners, Mirada | **Client:** IBM

The main aqueduct supplying New York City is dripping away a precious resource: water. Every two minutes, more than 20,000 gallons are lost.

Thanks to automated flow monitors and robotic inspections in the tunnel, the city can see precisely where the leaks are.

Now repairs are planned right where leaks occur.

Every day, enough water could be saved to fill 300,000 bathtubs.

15,000 gal

10,000 gal

5,000 gal

Assignment: More than 500 artifacts, all of which had been discovered at archaeological sites within Israel, provide visitors with a record of human achievement and clues to its people, their beliefs, and their way of life over the last three thousand years. Twenty Dead Sea Scrolls are featured in two rotations, and are displayed within a 25-foot-diameter communal table occupying the central gallery. Other design elements include a six-screen immersive introductory theater experience with a live narrator, a 100-foot-long reverse timeline (from present to past) showcasing iconic objects, a representation of an ancient Israelite house, and a three-ton stone from the Western Wall.

Approach: The exhibition space posed a number of challenges, mainly varied ceiling heights and a grid of large columns. The design team responded by using the area with a double-height ceiling for a dramatic reveal, and subsequent display, of the Dead Sea Scrolls. Columns were either hidden or became part of the exhibition's structure. Because the Dead Sea Scrolls are incredibly delicate, housing and display conditions are strict. The challenge was to meet these conditions and still create an immersive, emotionally evocative, and educational experience for visitors. The design solution was to create a white, 25-foot-diameter communal viewing table, whose contours are echoed by two arched stone walls that encircle the gallery. This exhibition presents a sophisticated story and complex information about the Dead Sea Scrolls' profound influence. The design breaks these into digestible chapters to ensure that visitors remain engaged. Clear, accessible, and inviting graphics support this effort.

Results: The design was an innovative approach to an exhibition about these extraordinary documents, in which the culture that created the Dead Sea Scrolls is portrayed as an essential element in understanding their continuing impact. The exhibition was well received by the public and is one of the largest touring collections of ancient artifacts from Israel, comprising more than 500 objects; it is also one of the largest loan displays of Dead Sea Scrolls (twenty, in two rotations).

Designer: Ralph Appelbaum Associates, Inc. | **Design Firm:** Ralph Appelbaum Associates, Inc. | **Client:** Running Subway

Assignment: To coincide with a packaging update, and a desire to fully articulate the proven performance values of BPTO 2197, Air BP Lubricants created a new communication toolkit with a focus on the lubricant's trusted performance for the modern generation of aviation turbine engines, including the Boeing Dreamliner 787.

Approach: The focus of the toolkit was a detailed rendering representative of the Rolls Royce Trent 1000 engine. An elegant level of technology detail was essential to reinforce the high-end positioning of a world leading product. The illustration was core to all communication channels and made available as a static image and 360-degree revolve animation sequence.

Results: These teams and their customers live and breath technology, so the new communications continue to be well received by our clients' technology and sales teams as a key support mechanism for customer conversations.

Designers: Neil Sims, Paul Ellis, Jim Meston | **Design Firm:** OMG (Oakwood Media Group) | **Client:** Air BP Lubricants

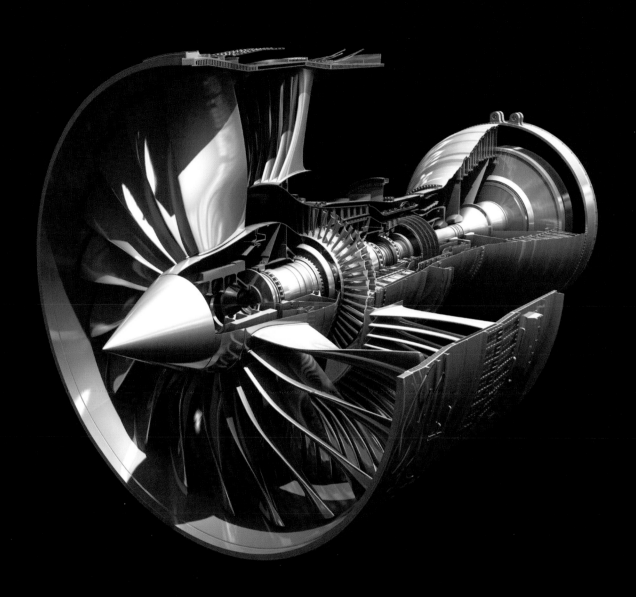

Assignment: The project was born as a collaboration with First Floor Under, an Italian creative blog. Our goal was to combine two things we deeply love: poetry and typography. We tried to create something that could speak the same language as the poem itself. The final result should bring you into the world the poet had in his mind (and in his heart): the passion, the feelings, the emotions. This–obviously–without adding a single word to the poem, but rather by using graphic design as an expressive tool.

Approach: For each poem, we tried to understand the historical moment, the subject, the author's personality, and the overall mood of the poem itself. Then, we tried to find an image and a typography that could convey that precise mood, which is something that can't be exactly described by words. We made a thorough research of fonts and images for each literary work. What was important to us was to create something that could help the beauty of the poem express itself and make you live for one moment in his imaginary world.

Results: The posters began to be posted in creative blogs and graphic design sites around the world. This brought a lot of contacts to our Web site, Facebook profile, and Vimeo page and greatly helped us to show our creative work, especially abroad.

Designers: Matteo Civaschi, Alessandra Miatello, Elena Scanferla, Sabine Troisvallets
Design Firm: H-57 Creative Station | **Client:** FirstFloorUnder.com

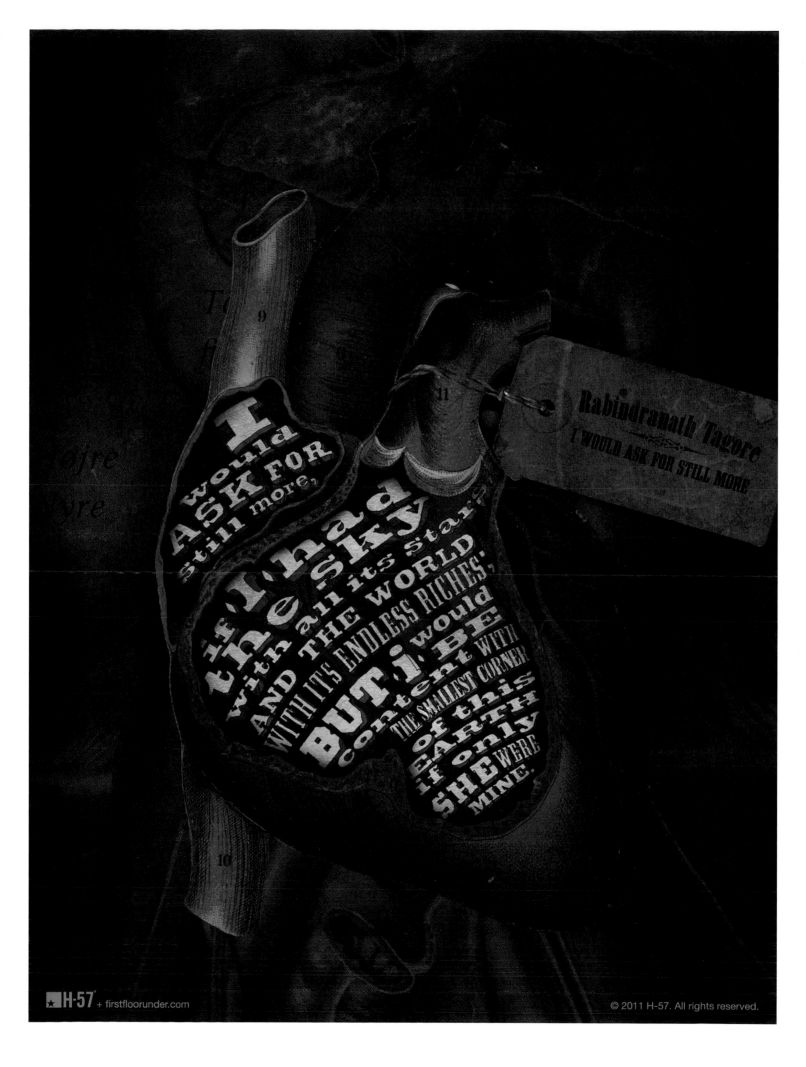

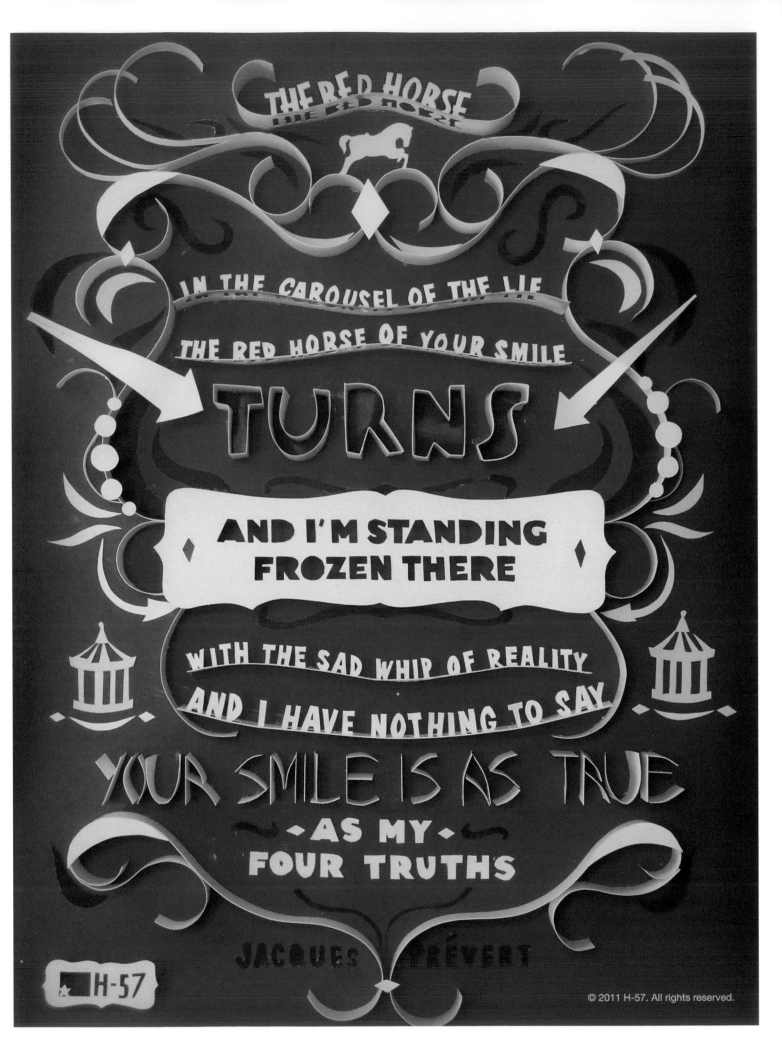

THE RED HORSE

IN THE CAROUSEL OF THE LIE
THE RED HORSE OF YOUR SMILE
TURNS
AND I'M STANDING FROZEN THERE
WITH THE SAD WHIP OF REALITY
AND I HAVE NOTHING TO SAY
YOUR SMILE IS AS TRUE
· AS MY ·
FOUR TRUTHS

JACQUES PRÉVERT

H-57

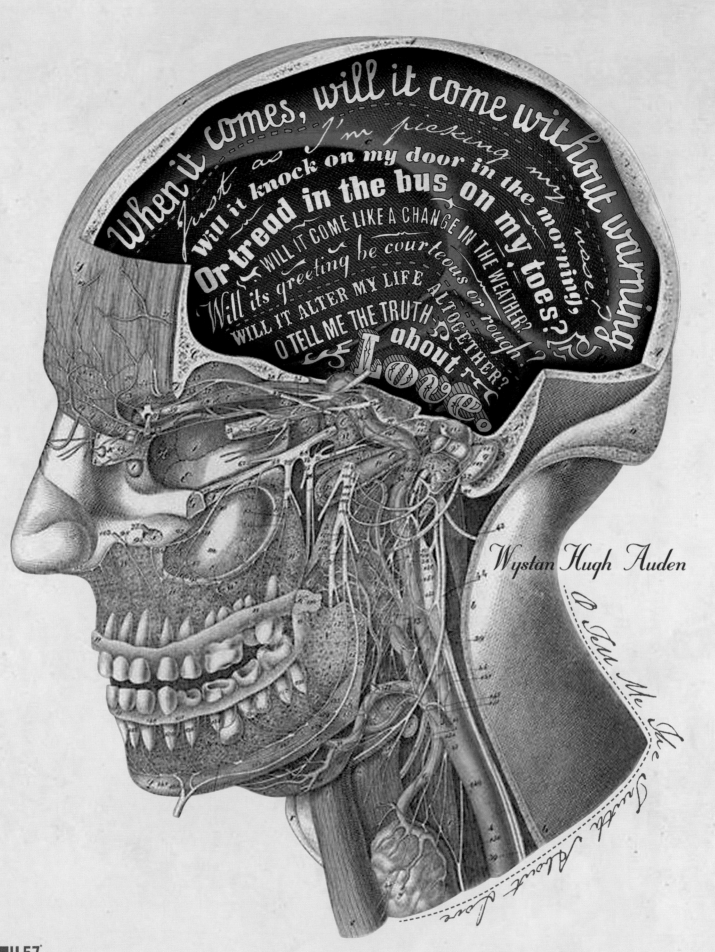

When it comes, will it come without warning
Just as I'm picking my nose?
Will it knock on my door in the morning,
Or tread in the bus on my toes?
Will it come like a change in the weather?
Will its greeting be courteous or rough?
Will it alter my life altogether?
O tell me the truth about Love.

Wystan Hugh Auden

Assignment: Honeywell wanted to evolve its traditional annual report to be an up-to-date central hub of information that could be accessed by anyone. We needed to provide a solution whereby Honeywell's communication platform would be as leading-edge as its own products and technologies.

Approach: The Honeywell Dashboard app for the iPad is designed to be the go-to source of information for the world of Honeywell, which users can browse at their own pace and filter the content to their own interests. It is continuously updated over the air and focuses on the Fortune 100 company's differentiated technologies, key process initiatives, strong financial performance, and alignment with global macro trends, such as safety, security, energy, and globalization. This app features current stock price information and company news along with hundreds of facts, statistics, animations, photos, and videos. In addition, we filmed, edited, and animated the CEO's annual message included in the app. Particularly fun and informative for every type of audience are the "Interactive Facts" embedded throughout the "Great Positions In Good Industries" section. We also launched a Flash Web version of the app to increase the Honeywell Dashboard's reach and access.

Results: Going forward, the client intends to update and refine the Dashboard quarterly and have it be the primary channel for its communication with investors and stakeholders.

Designer: Rick Slusher | **Design Firm:** Addison | **Client:** Honeywell

Assignment: Our brief—to create a brand that would position Matt Moran's new restaurant, Chiswick, as a relaxed neighborhood diner nestled in a unique, historic garden setting. The collateral includes all customer facing and corporate applications: signage, Web site, menu, wine list, uniforms, bill presenters, canvas tote bags, tea towels, coasters, and stationery.

Approach: Our creative solution was inspired by the site's historic gardens, and the recently planted 150–square–meter vegetable garden that will supply the restaurant with fresh produce.

Results: Every element of the design has a botanical influence—from the logo design featuring tendril-like typography, through to the soft muted palette, sustainable materials, and photographic studies of plants drawn from the gardens. The solution is elegant, sensual, and totally grounded in an appreciation of the natural elements that make the restaurant such a special place.

Designer: Vince Frost | **Design Firm:** Frost* Design | **Client:** Manfredi

CHISWICK

65 Ocean Street, Woollahra, NSW 2025
T: 02 8388 8688 F: 02 8388 8633
info@chiswickrestaurant.com.au
www.chiswickrestaurant.com.au

CHISWICK

65 Ocean Street, Woollahra, NSW 2025
T: 02 8388 8688 F: 02 8388 8633
info@chiswickrestaurant.com.au
www.chiswickrestaurant.com.au

Assignment: We were commissioned to create a new brand identity for Ray Man Photography. This renowned studio is the brainchild of Raymond Ng, one of Hong Kong's most celebrated advertising photographers and regarded as a guru among his peers.

Approach: In this brand identity, the initial "R" is formed by two parts: the letter "P" and a ray of light. The ray shines, reflects, and grows—symbolic of Raymond Ng's professional attitude of always exploring and developing possibilities to further enrich the creativity of his projects.

Design Firm: A Green Hill Communications Limited | **Art Director:** Nick Li | **Creative Director:** Raymond Tam | **Client:** Ray Man Photography

RayManPhotography
P
RayManPhotography
Raymond Ng
PHOTOGRAPHER
Joe Lam
PRODUCER
RayManPhotography
P
RayManPhotography

Assignment: For the 75th Anniversary of the Golden Gate Bridge in 2012, the Bridge Authority and the Golden Gate National Parks Conservancy needed a symbol to announce the celebratory event to the San Francisco Bay Area. The client wanted an icon to use in public spaces, retail merchandise, and various promotional materials.

Approach: We were inspired by the bridge's many iconic elements—the renowned International Orange color, the soaring towers of the suspension bridge, the Art Deco styling, and the sun's rays that shine through the bridge each evening at dusk. In addition to integrating these details into the design, we modified the de Stijl triangular points of the towers and repeated them around the logo to create a medallion-like border.

Designers: Kit Hinrichs, Gloria Hiek, Maurice Woods | **Design Firm:** Studio Hinrichs | **Client:** Golden Gate National Parks Conservancy

Assignment: Our assignment was to develop a brand identity for Manfredi's new restaurant, Balla, at The Star, Sydney. Named after the futurist poet and painter Giacomo Balla, this new restaurant seeks to redefine the classic Milanese osteria.

Approach: We took our inspiration and design influence from the Italian Futurist art movement, of which Milan was a major center in the early 20th century. Balla's depictions of light and speed were used as references for a custom-created typeface with its own sense of geometry and form.

Designers: Vince Frost, Graziela Machado | **Design Firm:** Frost* Design | **Client:** Manfredi

Assignment: Juma Ventures is a nonprofit organization providing at-risk teens the jobs and support they need to achieve the goal of attending college. Juma has a fantastic story but their branding never lived up to the power of their offering. Juma asked John McNeil Studio to create a new logo and brand positioning that matched their mission and the spirit of the youths in their program.

Approach: Juma's name comes from an African word meaning "work" or "gathering as a group of people." To help people with pronunciation, the logo has always featured a line over the "u." Where some saw a vowel stress, we saw a concept—a symbol for what these kids were doing every day: "raising the bar." The logo needed to appeal to a variety of audiences: corporate sponsors, donors, and (most importantly) the kids. The multiple bright colors were used to represent youth and multiculturalism, and to connote a brighter future for the kids.

Designer: Jure Gavran | **Design Firm:** John McNeil Studio | **Creative Directors:** Kim Le Liboux, John McNeil | **Client:** Juma Ventures

Assignment: The Wit & Wisdom logo was created for renowned chef Michael Mina for his new restaurant (a modern American tavern) in Baltimore, Maryland. The logo represents an updated approach to traditional early American tavern signboards and is implemented throughout all the restaurant's graphics.

Designers: Michael Vanderbyl, Kellie McCool | **Design Firm:** Vanderbyl Design | **Creative Director:** Michael Vanderbyl | **Client:** Mina Group

GOLDEN GATE BRIDGE 75TH ANNIVERSARY LOGO

Balla ID

JUMA

WIT & WISDOM

Assignment: Maud was tasked with designing the new identity, packaging, and print for start-up Edgeboard. These handmade chopping boards possess a special feature: an edge that you use to gather chopped-food and slide it off. The edge prevents the inevitable spill associated with traditional flat boards, and so became the key focus of the brand through naming and application.

Approach: The brandmark is based on this feature, and is only fully revealed when placed around a corner. In this way we were able to create a brand that truly reflects the product and its point of difference in the market, hopefully engineering a sense of discovery—that "aha!" moment that makes a identity stand out. The natural anti-bacterial, sustainable wood sourced form the Byron Shire is also used throughout packaging and stationery, further adding to the tactile impact of the product.

Designers: David Park, Hampus Jageland, Richard Smalley, Ben Crick | **Design Firm:** Maud | **Client:** Edgeboard

Assignment: The Marie Ferdinand Foundation is a non-profit mentor program based in San Antonio, Texas, that is dedicated to teaching young girls to become strong women. Basketball is a central component to develop character and sportsmanship. We were approached to redesign their current logo.

Approach: Our client required a graphic solution to quickly convey that the program was for girls and primarily centered around basketball. While looking at a simple photograph of a basketball, the solution revealed itself.

Designers: Bradford Lawton, Josue Zapata | **Design Firm:** BradfordLawton | **Client:** Marie Ferdinand Foundation

Assignment: Established in 2008, Indiegogo has become a pioneer and innovator in the crowd-funding space and has had a huge impact on how people around the world fund their own ideas. Due to their impressive growth, they felt it was time to take their brand identity and Web site to the next level; a level that felt more established, friendly, and modern; a level that felt like they'd arrived on the global stage. Most importantly, the logo needed to visually communicate Indiegogo's core values: collaboration, inspiration, independent spirit, and passion.

Approach: Before we started the creative design process, we studied. Through research, customer surveys, and competitive analysis, we discovered that their brand essence and positioning were based around the ideas of personal empowerment and inspiration on a global scale. We now had a solid foundation to establish visual concepts—the fun part. After an extensive brand exploratory, we developed these multi-colored, interwoven shapes that reflected the collaborative nature of their platform. These shapes also represent their diverse community, where ideas come together and form something that is much larger than the sum of its parts. We chose bright, happy colors that represent diversity and that stand out among the competition. We also felt that the mark could be seen in different ways to different people. There are heart shapes that represent passion, woven shapes that represent collaboration, and an atomic shape representing energy and thought. All aspects of the visual identity from the mark to the Web site were carefully chosen to help Indiegogo achieve a more inviting user and brand experience, establishing them as a global player.

Designers: Adam Goldberg, Monika Kehrer | **Design Firm:** TRÜF | **Client:** Indiegogo

Assignment: Although we had been building sites for our clients on our own proprietary CMS, Point & Clique, for years, we were still known largely for design and not technology. So, when we launched our version 6 of Point & Clique, we needed an image that hinted at its force in the CMS universe.

Approach: V6 Sounded like a car model, so what better way to convey its power and speed than a sleek racing car and a logo resembling a luxury car emblem? Thus, the V6 campaign was born.

Results: With the V6 logo, we now have a face in the technology industry and have since gained a larger presence in the sphere than we had previously.

Designers: Burkey Belser, Mark Ledgerwood | **Design Firm:** Greenfield/Belser, Ltd. | **Client:** Greenfield/Belser, Ltd.

MARIE FERDINAND FOUNDATION

INDIEGOGO

POINT & CLIQUE V6

162 FEED IT LOGOS GOLD

Assignment: We set out to create an icon for an inspirational speaking series that hosts well-known people from the worlds of marketing, digital, and entertainment.

Approach: We wanted to keep the icon simple and bold, but also wanted it to communicate that the speaking series provides a lot of good information and new ways of looking at things in the world of business.

Designer: Andrew Wetzel | **Design Firm:** Colle+McVoy | **Executive Creative Director:** Mike Caguin | **Client:** Colle+McVoy

162 MR. COOK IDENTITY LOGOS GOLD

Assignment: To create a brand identity for Mr. Cook and distinguish him as the new name in floral design in Sydney, Australia.

Approach: This project was a very personal one for the client and we worked with him closely to capture his strong aesthetic and his approach to his work. We interpreted his "organic luxe" style as a series of floral explosions that define the exuberance and artistry of Mr. Cook flowers and reflect the sensory experience of being in the store amongst them. We created the identity as an ongoing series, as the flowers are always changing, unexpected, and truly gorgeous. We developed the new brand through stationery, gift cards, wrapping design, store interior, signage, and the Web site, www.mrcook.com.au.

Designers: Vanessa Ryan, Wendy Cho | **Design Firm:** SML | **Client:** Mr. Cook

162 THINAIRE CORPORATE IDENTITY LOGOS GOLD

Assignment: thinaire is a transmedia technology that empowers people to touch their NFC-enabled mobile phones to print media and other physical objects, launching a thin-client application that enables infinite interaction and engagement with brands, retailers, friends, and causes. thinaire required a logo that was as elegant and as simple as its solution.

Designer: Drew Allison | **Design Firm:** Drew Allison: Brand Expression | **Client:** thinaire

162 LÆRDAL GRØNT LOGO GOLD

Assignment: Lærdal is placed in the Sognefjord area of Norway, considered one of the world's most beautiful destinations. Lærdal Grønt needed to go from being a small local producer to establishing itself as a premium supplier of vegetables and large tasty cherries for the European market.

Approach: Strømme Throndsen Design developed an organic logo and visual identity for Lærdal Grønt, with the aim of pursuing Lærdal Grønt as an independent and strong premium brand. The visual identity communicates tasty delicacy through the use of smooth and clean typography and natural colors.

Results: The client received a significant increase in both sales and awareness.

Designer: Morten Throndsen | **Design Firm:** Strømme Throndsen Design | **Client:** Lærdal Grønt

FEED IT

MR COOK IDENTITY

THINAIRE CORPORATE IDENTITY

LÆRDAL GRØNT

LÆRDAL GRONT

Assignment: When it came to branding WURST, the initial challenge lay in creating an identity that worked for two unique spaces within the same establishment—an upscale restaurant upstairs and a raucous beer hall downstairs.

Approach: To do so, we combined traditional German elements and flipped many of them on their heads, giving WURST a sophisticated, yet playful feel. We chose the restaurant/beer hall's name because sausage is featured so heavily on the menu, and because it sounds like worst, and who in their right mind would name their restaurant something like that? The logo leans on classic German imagery with a modern twist, featuring a two-headed eagle holding a bratwurst and stein, one side refined and one side tipsy. Two typefaces were used for the coasters, menu, and signage: Futura and Fette Fraktur. Both German, one a modern and sleek sans serif, balanced by a traditional blackletter font.

Results: The identity was well received by both the client and the general public. WURST just celebrated its first birthday and there are lines extending out the door every weekend.

Designers: Theresa Kwan, Hans Thiessen | **Design Firm:** WAX | **Client:** WURST

BEER
DRAFT
BOTTLED
BEER COCKTAILS

COCKTAILS

MARTINIS

WINE
WHITE
SPARKLING
RED

Beer

DRAFT

CRISP & CLEAN	200 ml	½ Litre	1 Litre	2L Boot
WURST 1516, Lager, Canada				
WURSTER Kolsch, Lager, Canada	3	8.5	17	30
Budweiser, Lager, USA	3	8.5	17	30
Becks, Pilsner, Germany	3	6.5	13	30
Pilsner Urquell, Pilsner, Czech	4	9	18	-
Stiegl, Lager, Austria	4	9	18	-
Warsteiner Premium Verum, Pilsner, Germany	4	0	18	-

PALES & ALES				
FRANZL'S Roggen, Ale, Canada	4	9	18	
Keith's Indian Pale, Ale, Canada	3	8.5	17	30
Big Rock Traditional, Ale, Canada	3	7.5	15	30
Koning Shoeven Tripel, Ale, Netherlands	3	7.5	15	

WHEATY & YEASTY				
Ayinger Brau Weiss, Wheat Beer, Germany	4	11.5	21	-
Konig Ludwig Weissbier, Wheat Beer, Germany	4	10.5	21	-
Erdinger Weissbier, Wheat Beer, Germany	4	10.5	21	-
	4	10.5		

RED, BLACK & BROWN				
WURSTEST Dunkel, Dark Lager, Canada				
Alexander Keith's Red, Red Ale, Canada	3	8.5	17	30
Ayinger Celebrator Doppelbock, Dark Lager, Germany	3	7.5	15	30
Warsteiner Dunkel, Dark Lager, Germany	4	11.5	21	-
Erdinger Dunkel, Wheat Beer, Germany	4	9.5	19	-
	4	9.5	19	-

FRUITS & CIDERS				
Sir Perry Pear Cider, Pear Cider, England	4	9	18	-

✦✦✦✦✦

THE GERMAN PURITY LAW OF 1516 (REINHEITSGEBOT)

A regulation covering the production of beer in Germany based upon Bavarian custom. It allows for the production of beer with three ingredients—water, barley and hops. It was later revised to allow yeast.

There are two types of beer in the world:

ALE—beer brewed from malted barley using warm top fermentation and generally contain hops to help preserve the beer and balance the flavor. Ales are generally stronger than lagers.

LAGER—a bottom fermented beer brewed from malted barley. There are three styles of Lager; a light and effervescent version, a dark Lager called Dunkles and a pale version called Pilsner.

BOTTLED

CRISP & CLEAN		
Coors Light, Lager, USA	335 ml	5.5
Kokanee, Lager, Canada	335 ml	5.5
Lowenbrau, Lager, Munich	500 ml	9
Bud Light Lime, Lager, USA	335 ml	6
Dab Original, Pilsner, Germany	330 ml	6
Bavaria, Pilsner, Holland	330 ml	6
He'Brew Genesis, Lager, USA	330 ml	7

PALES & ALES		
Les Trois Mousquetaires Imperial Weizen, Pale Ale, Canada	750 ml	18.5
Les Trois Mousquetaires Sticke Alt, Ale, Canada	750 ml	18.5
Greens Amber (Gluten Free), Ale, Belgium	335 ml	14

WHEATY & YEASTY		
Hacker-Pschorr Weisse, Wheat Beer, Germany	500 ml	9
Pinkus-Muller Organic, Pilsner, Germany	500 ml	11
Pinkus-Muller Alt, Wheat Beer, Germany	500 ml	11
Hacker-Pschorr Edelhell, Lager, Germany	500 ml	9
Weihenstephaner Hefeweissbier Dunkel (the world's oldest Brewery), Dark Wheat Beer, Germany	500 ml	11

FRUITS & CIDERS		
Schofferhofer Grapefruit, 50/50 Wheat Beer & Real Grapefruit Juice, Germany	330 ml	6.5
Blackthorn Cider, Apple Cider, England	500 ml	6.5
Mikes Hard Lemonade, Vodka Cooler, Canada	330 ml	5.5
Mikes Hard Cranberry, Vodka Cooler, Canada	330 ml	5.5

NON ALCOHOLIC		
Erdinger Lager, Germany, 0.5%	500 ml	5.5
Becks, Lager, Germany, 0.5%	355 ml	5.5

BEER COCKTAILS   ½ Litre

Beer in a Bag *Tall Boy of Lowenbrau in a Brown Paper Bag with a Shot of Goldschläger*	16
The Black & White *Ayinger Celebrator Doppelbock & Ayinger Brau Weiss*	10
Snake Bite *Pilsner Urquell & Sir Perry Cider*	10
Traditional Float *Big Rock Traditional Ale & Sir Perry Cider*	10
WURST Shandy *WURST 1516 & 7up*	10
Cream of Wheat *King Ludwig Weissbier & Franzl's Roggen*	10
Guten Tag Red Eye *Budweiser & Clamato*	10
Hahnenkamm *Stiegl & Shot of Jägermeister*	16

✦✦✦✦✦

TRAY OF BEER

Tray of Kolsch Beer (8) 200 ml	24
Flügel Flight (4) 200 ml *Becks, Warsteiner Premium Verum, Konig Ludwig Weissbier, Erdinger Dunkel*	16
Whacky Wheats (3) 200 ml *Erdinger Weissbier, Ayinger Weiss, Konig Ludwig Weissbier*	12
Create Your Own Tray (4) 200 ml	16

✦✦✦✦✦

COCKTAILS   2 oz/9.5

Die Besten WURST Caesar
42 Below Vodka, Lee and Perrins, Tabasco, Celery Salted Rim
Customize your Caesar with Two of the Following –
Dash of Horseradish, Smoked Bison Wurst, Pickle,
Celery Stick, Pickled Beet, Olive Skewer, Smoked Tomato
Ketchup, Sea Salt Rim, Steak Salt Rim

Cuckoo Cocktail
Raspberry Stoli, Raspberry Puree, Sparkling Wine

WURST Mojito
Bacardi Rum, Muddled Mint & Lime, Brown Simple Syrup, Soda, Lime Juice

Einstein Rose Sangria
Rose wine, Lemonade, Boozy Berries, Sprite

Beethoven Spritzer
Van Gogh Caramel Vodka, Sauvignon Blanc, Apple Juice, Soda

Beerhall Margarita
Cazadores Tequila, Grand Martini, Cream, Fresh Lime Juice, Salted Rim

✦✦✦✦✦

MARTINIS   2 oz/11

The Black Forest
Cherry Brandy, Grand Marnier, Raspberry Vodka, Van Gogh Dutch Chocolate

Freudian Slip
Cherry Brandy, Grand Marnier, Sparkling Wine Fresh Lemon Juice

Oom Pah Pah Pom
Raspberry Vodka, Grand Marnier, POM Juice

$E=MC^2$
Van Gogh Espresso Vodka, Kahlua, Baileys, Milk

Blue Dog
42 Below Vodka, Blue Curacao, Fresh Lemon Juice

WURST DRINKS
JULY 2011

Assignment: The aim was to establish Jens Eide as a specialist, offering handcrafted taste and a wide variety of meat and sausages. The design was based upon the values of competence, quality, local production, and pride and has resulted in a simple, however powerful design that encompasses the idea "Butcher-handcrafted from the heart of Agder in Norway."

Approach: Strømme Throndsen Design wanted the craftsmanship to be easily visible in a category dominated by big industrial brands. The packaging, which is completely honest and straightforward, aims to show the company's quality and passion. The profile text tells the story of skilled quality craftsmanship in an honest and charming way, and the inside reveals realistically clear photos of the food.

Results: The client reports a reinvigorated energy in the company and among the employees. In the first year after relaunch, Jens Eide sold 46,000 retail packs for supermarkets, which was double the number of consumer units from the year before.

Designers: Eia Grødal, Morten Throndsen | **Design Firm:** Strømme Throndsen Design | **Client:** Butcher Jens Eide

Din lokale slakter

LILLESAND · SØRLANDET

VÅRT MÅL er det samme nå, som da vi grunnla bedriften i 1946: Vi vil bidra til *trivsel ved matbordet!* Og god mat skaper trivsel, mener vi. Vi setter vår ære i at produktkvaliteten alltid skal være den ypperste, og SMAKEN DEN ALLER BESTE. Derfor selger vi kun mørt kvalitetskjøtt fra *lokale bønder i Agder.* Det samme møre kjøttet bruker vi i alle våre produkter; TRADISJONSRIK SPEKEMAT, KNALLGODE PØLSER, SPENNENDE PATÉER og *smakfullt* PÅLEGG. Handler du hos oss, er *veien til et velsmakende måltid kort.*

PØLSEMAKEREN ANBEFALER

Bratwürst

Grovhakket pølse med karve

EKTE HANDVERKSPØLSER UTVIKLET GJENNOM GENERASJONER · PRISBELØNNET SMAK ·

VÅRT MÅL er det samme nå, som da vi grunnla bedriften i 1946: Vi vil bidra til *trivsel ved matbordet!* Og god mat skaper trivsel, mener vi. Vi setter vår ære i at produktkvaliteten alltid skal være den ypperste, og SMAKEN DEN ALLER BESTE. Derfor selger vi kun mørt kvalitetskjøtt fra *lokale bønder i Agder.* Det samme møre kjøttet bruker vi i alle våre produkter; TRADISJONSRIK SPEKEMAT, KNALLGODE PØLSER, SPENNENDE PATÉER og *smakfullt* PÅLEGG. Handler du hos oss, er *veien til et velsmakende måltid kort.*

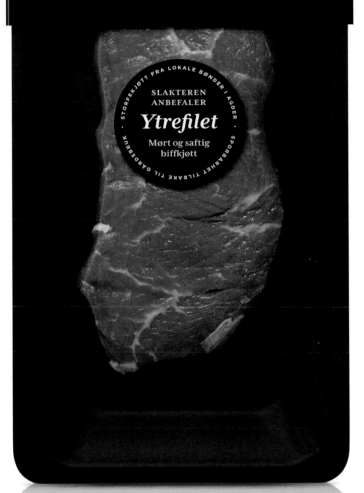

SLAKTEREN ANBEFALER

Ytrefilet

Mørt og saftig biffkjøtt

STORFEKJØTT FRA LOKALE BØNDER I AGDER · SPORBARHET TILBAKE TIL GÅRDSBRUK ·

Assignment: A little known liqueur with Italian roots and strong taste appeal, Tuaca was often overlooked on the shelf due to its lacking an understandable persona. Instead, the brand relied on bartenders and word of mouth to validate its credibility. Described as easy to love and easy to share, Tuaca is a bridge to new friends and adventure—but the old design was anything but adventurous. The opportunity for Tuaca: create a new, higher energy persona for a premium spirit that invites consumers to step beyond the familiar.

Approach: Italian design sensibilities inspired a design that is bolder, timeless, and inviting. The new design sheds the old without throwing away elements of its rich heritage and story. Tuaca is a liqueur with a taste that's highly mixable and open to almost any occasion. New branding makes it appealing to an audience that's open to trying new things in new ways. Consumed primarily as a shot, the product is exceptionally flexible—it can be consumed straight or mixed, cold or warm, sweet or sour. The new design is inspired by that variety and created to deliver a dynamic, inviting persona. To be relevant, brands need to get noticed, speak in a consistent voice, and engage in interesting ways. More and more, brands are activated at the local level. To provide tools and communicate with the field, we created the Tuaca brand activation guide. It provides branding elements and programs packaged in a cool, Tuaca way.

Results: The new brand identity and package are more visible, compelling, and energetic. And, the package more accurately represents the product's taste profile. The extended identity system encourages more interesting engagement with a "kit of parts" that can be used in a variety of ways. Qualitative research has validated the new identity and label design for the brand. Consumers recognize the product as more premium and relevant, and it has grown through a reinvigorated promotional effort.

Designers: Kate Arends, Alan Colvin **| Design Firm:** Cue **| Client:** Brown-Forman

Assignment: Range of very exclusive wines, with numbered production up to 6,000 bottles.

Approach: The label embraces the bottle almost fully, using typography as its main visual element. It is full of small texts like vinification and tasting notes, harvest information, *terroir*, grape variety, and GPS coordinates. Being a very technically controlled wine, in this label, ornament is information.

Designer: Eduardo Aires | **Design Firm:** White Studio | **Client:** Esporão

Assignment: This John Varvatos Star USA project challenged YARD to translate the Star USA tier for fragrance licensee Elizabeth Arden, while staying true to the innovative approach to branding of the John Varvatos fragrance portfolio and allowing the new Star USA packaging to live alongside the existing John Varvatos Collection fragrance tier.

Approach: For the Star USA fragrance project, YARD articulated a brand muse, "The artistically rebellious visionary who is not a wannabe but an about-to-be"—who inspired the creation of the innovative fragrance bottle. The design also drew inspiration from poison vials from the 1800s, old beer bottles, military equipment, and the industrial details YARD has made a signature of the Varvatos brand. The use of the hinged cap was designed to preserve a strong presence at retail, since fragrance tester bottles often lose their caps, and with them their branding.

Results: The John Varvatos Star USA fragrance was awarded the prestigious 2012 Fifi for Best Men's Luxe Packaging.

Designers: Stephen Niedzwiecki, David Calderly | **Design Firm:** YARD | **Client:** John Varvatos Star USA

Assignment: Our client tasked us with continuing the success of the previous two summers to once again communicate "Coca-Cola refreshes summer fun." The designs needed to use the iconic Coca-Cola visual language to form a natural connection between the joy and optimism of the brand and the summer season. The graphics created would be featured on packaging, in-store displays, and premium merchandise, all in celebration of summer's favorite beverage—Coca-Cola.

Approach: We focused on the special moments of summer, and Coca-Cola's authentic connection to the season. Coca-Cola is particularly popular at summer picnics, so we created a picnic basket using Coca-Cola iconography. The shape of the graphic naturally filled the format of the packaging, therefore creating the illusion of carrying a Coca-Cola picnic basket when brought home from the grocery store.

Designer: Brian Steele | **Design Firm:** Turner Duckworth Design: London & San Francisco
Creative Directors: David Turner, Bruce Duckworth, Sarah Moffat | **Client:** The Coca-Cola Company North America

Assignment: Coca-Cola and World Wildlife Fund (WWF) joined forces in a bold new initiative to help protect the polar bear's Arctic home. Coca-Cola committed up to $3 million to WWF's conservation efforts, and planned an "Arctic Home" campaign to achieve the following:
- Increase brand love
- Provide retail excitement for winter months
- Demonstrate Coca-Cola's commitment to "Live Positively"
- Stay at the forefront of marketing innovation

To galvanize fans to help donate, Coca-Cola turned its iconic red cans white, and partnered with us to create the visual graphics that informed the packaging and campaign identity.

Approach: Our goal was to bring awareness to the Arctic Home cause and invite consumers to join Coca-Cola and WWF in helping to protect the polar bear by featuring its image prominently on packaging. The graphics would be applied to all Coca-Cola packaging SKUs.

The familiar red can background was replaced with an all-white panorama, highlighted by the iconic Coca-Cola script printed in red.

The eye-catching cans featured the image of a mother bear and her two cubs making their way across the Arctic. The complementary red can featured the same illustrations on a red background in celebration of the holiday season. We then extended the concept to a range of packaging, including the fridgepack.

Results: The project has shown increases in key measures: Coca-Cola brand health measures, volumes, and social media positive mentions.

Designer: Butler Looney | **Design Firm:** Turner Duckworth Design: London & San Francisco
Creative Directors: David Turner, Bruce Duckworth, Sarah Moffat | **Client:** The Coca-Cola Company North America

24 cans

Coca-Cola

· Coca-Cola ·

24-12 FL OZ CANS (288 FL OZ) 24-355 mL CANS (8.52 L)

140 CALORIES PER CAN

Coca-Cola

12 FL OZ (355 mL)

Coca-Cola®

140 CALORIES PER CAN

12 cans

Coca-Cola®

12-12 FL OZ CANS (144 FL OZ)
12-355 mL CANS (4.26 L)

140 CALORIES | 0g SAT FAT | 45mg SODIUM | 39g SUGARS
PER SERVING 1 CAN

JOIN COCA-COLA AND **WORLD WILDLIFE FUND** IN OUR EFFORT TO PROTECT THE POLAR BEAR'S HOME.

To donate $1, find your code inside and details on back.

Approach: Aimed at professional recording engineers and passionate audiophiles, the sumptuous, close-up photography highlights every nuance of the product, suggesting the detailed sound quality it delivers.

Designer: Angela Renac | **Design Firm:** MiresBall | **Creative Director:** John Ball | **Photographer:** Marc Tule
Account Supervisor: Holly Houk **Client:** Shure

176 SHURE ULTRA-PREMIUM HEADPHONES PACKAGING **GOLD**

Assignment: The goal was to launch a high-end rye whiskey, which was the first offering from a new spirits company, 35 Maple Street. The reputation of this new company rested largely on the success of this first spirit. While high-end whiskeys were well established in the market, rye whiskey represented a more traditional type of whiskey that had fallen out of fashion amid excitement about bourbons and single malt scotch. Rye whiskey has been undergoing a resurgence among aficionados, so the timing of our launch was excellent. That said, the expectations of the high-end whiskey drinker are great, so it was essential that the look of the bottle, label, and packaging reflected the quality of the liquid inside.

Approach: Rye whiskey is a very traditional American whiskey. In the 1800s and early 1900s, a large portion of the whiskey consumed was rye whiskey. It was the classic drink consumed by dusty, thirsty cowboys in the Old West; in fact, a lot of the ingredients that went into the distillation process were from the West. We drew inspiration from the Americana aspect of the drink. Combined with the fact that rye whiskey was a fairly unique and high-end offering, this eventually led us to a concept that represented unique, quality and western–the Old West Renaissance man, Bat Masterson. We brought the Masterson concept to life in a number of ways. The packaging is imbued with Bat Masterson's life and lore. The bottle has a strikingly graceful shoulder that's reminiscent of 19th's century whiskey flasks, while the small front label lets the whiskey's glorious amber hue do most of the talking. Serving as a tribute to Masterson's days as a renowned journalist, the die-cut label resembles a clipped-out newspaper column, complete with torn edges like a real newspaper. The exterior box features a die-cut window, allowing the label to stand out, yet also fit in seamlessly with the newspaper articles printed over the surface of the box. The articles, which delve deeper into Masterson's life, were custom written in the distinctively verbose and dramatic turn-of-the-century tone.

Results: 35 Maple Street Spirits was very pleased with the outcome, and they, in fact, became Bat Masterson fans themselves, attending industry events wearing Bat Masterson's trademark bowler hat. The whiskey sold very well while receiving critical acclaim and high ratings from numerous spirits experts. Having sold out their first batch, they are excited about a second run of the whiskey, which is currently in the works.

Designers: Sallie Reynolds Allen | **Design Firm:** Studio 32 North | **Client:** 35 Maple Street Spirits

Assignment: Develop a brand identity for Manfredi's new restaurant, Balla, at The Star, Sydney. Named after the futurist poet and painter Giacomo Balla, this new restaurant seeks to redefine the classic Milanese osteria. The project included the creation of a bespoke font, menus, coasters, letterhead, an olive bottle, wine app, and signage.

Approach: We took our inspiration and design influence from the Italian Futurist art movement, of which Milan was a major center in the early 20th century. Balla's depictions of light and speed were used as references for a custom-created typeface with its own sense of geometry and form.

Results: The striking typography and colors redefine traditional associations with Italian restaurants, preparing patrons for a gastronomic experience like no other. The dramatic graphic language of geometric shapes evoke the classic, urban style of Milan, creating a restaurant identity that defines the Manfredi patron's expectations of fine Italian dining in today's world.

Designers: Vince Frost, Graziela Machado | **Design Firm:** Frost* Design | **Client:** Manfredi

EXTRA VIRGIN

OLIVE OIL

750ml

BALLA

Assignment: As part of The Glenlivet brand redesign we were asked to update the Nàdurra to communicate the unique and highly individual character of the whisky.

Approach: Taking inspiration from the unadulterated nature of the whisky, all elements of the design—from the handcrafted "Nàdurra" type to the stenciling featured on the carton and tissue wrap—were developed to reference this highly crafted and individual whisky, a purer expression of The Glenlivet's great tradition.

Designers: David Blakemore, Clem Halpin | **Design Firm:** Turner Duckworth Design: London & San Francisco
Design Director: Clem Halpin | **Creative Directors:** David Turner, Bruce Duckworth | **Client:** Chivas Brothers Ltd.

Assignment: The brief was to design and launch the new Tom Ford beauty line. It needed to communicate an extension of the Tom Ford vision, while being unique and bold within the crowded high-end beauty world. The challenge was in creating a new design vocabulary that could be scalable across an entire range of products, from bottles to tubes and brushes, all in varying materials, sizes, and uses.

Approach: Tom Ford has a very distinct design sensibility and our role was to distill his vision into a distinct packaging program that would align both Tom Ford and Estee Lauder, the licensor. Further to that, it is understanding the consumer in this category and ensuring that we are delivering a design that inspires them to purchase the product. Our experience in beauty lends a strong focus that allows us to do just that.

Results: The client is extremely happy with the end result and has continued to add additional SKU's to the initial lineup.

Designers: Doug Lloyd, Asako Aeba | **Design Firm:** LLOYD&CO | **Client:** Tom Ford

Assignment: This Isopure project challenged YARD to create stronger brand recognition and a cohesive packaging collection for their products, consisting of drinks, powders, and vitamins.

Approach: To accomplish this, YARD created a strategic platform titled "We're All More Than Muscle," which would inspire all creative executions, including packaging. YARD transformed Isopure's dated look by simplifying the portfolio hierarchy, while introducing a more modern design sensibility and color system.

Results: As a result, brand recognition was strengthened at the retail level, and the positive reception led to new retail opportunities with GNC and the Vitamin Shoppe. Isopure CEO, Hal Katz remarked, "April 2011 was the best month in the history of the Isopure company with sales up 20%. I attribute this success to the new Isopure packaging that YARD has created."

Designers: Stephen Niedzwiecki, Amber Chandler | **Design Firm:** YARD | **Client:** Isopure

Assignment: March is a retail store in San Francisco that features provisions for the hearth and home. We designed the identity and packaging system for March Pantry, the label for the seasonal and limited-production goods that March carries.

Results: The packaging is a favorite on Pinterest.

Designers: Angie Wang, Mark Fox | **Design Firm:** Design is Play | **Client:** MARCH

Assignment: We were asked to redesign and reinvent this product, to change the perception of the brand, making it appeal to a younger audience, to increase the brand's Celtic heritage, and to ultimately make the product jump off the shelf.

Approach: Our approach is simple: find out as much as we can about our client, as well as the brand we are working on, and look for the unique qualities in both; then, through interaction, build something unique that answers the task set before us.

Designer: Marcus Klim | **Design Firm:** Klim Design, Inc. | **Client:** Castle Brands, Inc.

Assignment: The agency was tasked with developing the entire brand identity (logo, graphics, packaging, and overall store look and feel) for a new, one-of-a-kind dessert boutique in New Orleans, Louisiana.

Approach: A clash between Americana and contemporary diners, designs were kept simple with pastel color palettes. The packaging designs were inspired by French-influenced and Southern-charmed candy shops.

Results: They look sweeeeeet.

Design Firm: Peter Mayer Advertising | **Senior Art Director:** Missy Dalton | **Creative Director:** Neil Landry | **Client:** Sucre

Assignment: Bottle Tree Beverage Co. invited HOOK to design a handsome bottle as a wedding gift to the Bristow Family.

Approach: We wanted this brand new gin to fit seamlessly on Grandfather Bristow's bar. It needed to look authentic, timeless, and tough. Looking back through the family's heirlooms, we discovered the crest and "Bristow" calligraphy. Both helped capture the essence of this old English family. Any additional colors felt complicated and frivolous. The stark black and white color palette maximized contrast and reinforced the masculine design. To add depth to the two-color design, the crest was printed on the back side of the bottle to read straight through the perfectly clear gin. The bottle number and date are handwritten on each label, a reminder of its small-batch quality and excellence. The gin now proudly stands in Grandfather Bristow's bar as the newest family heirloom. The back of the bottle shares the story of Bristow Gin:

"In exchange for his granddaughter's hand in marriage, a curious young bloke presented his new grandfather-in-law, Judge, with a bottle of gin. The gin was triple distilled with a curious blend of spices. The Judge was tickled by the gin and insisted his grandson-in-law provide him with a regular allocation of the toothsome spirit. With that encouraging nod, Bristow Gin was born and went on to live most happily ever after. Carefully made in small batches with eleven botanicals to give the Judge's gin a clearly unique and satisfying character."

Results: Bristow Gin was featured in *Food & Wine Magazine*'s list of America's Best New Gins, and on design blogs Lovely Package and DesignWorkLife.

Designers: Trish Ward, Brady Waggoner | **Design Firm:** HOOK | **Client:** Bottle Tree Beverage Company

VIGILANTIBU

Bristow

TRIPLE DISTILLED **GIN** 47% ALC/VOL 94 PROOF

APRIL 14, 2012 — BR — THIRTY NINE
BOTTLING DATE   BOTTLE NUMBER

Assignment: This is a "sweets and coffee" shop that carries out both activities at 50%. The corporate image and packaging is divided equally between brown (symbolizing the coffee) and different basic colors (symbolizing sweets).

Design Firm: Bisgràfic | **Client:** La Nevateria

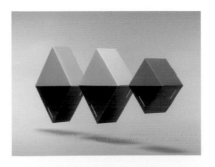

Assignment: This poster was designed as a promotional and marketing tool to promote *AS IF Magazine* to potential purchasers and advertisers. It was sent to advertisers and directors and used as takeaway at magazine launch events.

Approach: IF Studio's approach to the design of the magazine was to be completely non-formulaic and design each image and graphic to relate only to the specific story's editorial content. When designing the poster, we chose imagery that represented the strength and simplicity of the magazine's concept, making sure that it reflected creativity in many fields such as design, beauty, fashion, architecture, photography, filmmaking ... even music and food.

Results: Although quantifiable or monetized results from the poster promotion cannot be quoted, the poster was very well received—everyone wanted one and some were even "stolen" from events and launch parties!

Designers: Toshiaki Ide, Hisa Ide | **Design Firm:** IF Studio | **Photographer:** Tatijana Shoan | **Client:** AS IF Magazine
Editor in Chief: Tatijana Shoan

Assignment: The School of Visual Arts has been creating posters for New York City subway platforms for decades. The posters are familiar to all straphangers and have become a part of the culture of NYC. SVA's goal is to continually commission new artists and designers to create something unique that will bring attention to the school and its excellence.

Approach: From Louise Fili's blog: "The design is an homage to the urban mosaic artisans of the early 20th century, and after hours of painstaking Photoshop work, John and Dana agreed that it may have been easier to create it out of actual tiles."

Designers: Louise Fili, John Passafiume, Dana Tanamachi | **Design Firm:** Louise Fili, Ltd. | **Client:** School of Visual Arts

IT'S NEVER TOO LATE TO GET WHERE YOU'RE GOING

SCHOOL OF VISUAL ARTS

SVA.EDU
DESIGN BY LOUISE FILI LTD

Assignment: The poster was created to remember and to raise community awareness to encourage donations after Japan's March 11, 2011, earthquake and subsequent tsunami.

Approach: Synthesis, emphasis, and drama.

Results: In a few hours after the online publication the poster was shared thousands of times in the main social networks and on hundreds of blogs and sites, including *Osocio*, *Graffica*, and *Vogue*.

The poster has also been published in the Polish magazine *Exklusiv* and was exhibited in several cities such as:

• International Poster Exhibition, Imam Ali Museum of Arts, Teheran, Iran

• ACT Responsible Expo at Cannes Lions, 58th International Festival of Creativity, Cannes, France

• International Poster Exhibition, Iran Art Organization, Teheran, Iran

• Project Sunshine for Japan, Japanese House, Düsseldorf, Germany

• Green+You Posters for Japan Exhibition, Doosung In the paper Gallery, Seoul, Korea

It was selected as a winner for Project Sunshine for Japan and Green+You Posters for Japan. The poster was also sold at auction in Germany to raise money for the Red Cross.

Designers: Andrea Castelletti | **Design Firm:** Andrea Castelletti | **Client:** Help Japan

11/03/11

11/03/11

Assignment: Part of an experimental project continuously focused on expanding 2D types into a 3D environment.
The poster is designed for the 4th Project: "Unstable Unity."

Approach: Converting 2D types into 3D imagery in terms of expanding visualization possibilities.

Designer: Hoon-Dong Chung | **Design Firm:** Dankook University

3D TYPOGRAPHY EXHIBITION

EXPERIMENT WITH
SPATIAL ENVIRONMENTS

THE FINAL PART OF THE UNSTABLE UNITY

4TH WORKS
DECEMBER 23 2011

CREATED BY
HOONDONG CHUNG
DANKOOK UNIVERSITY

Assignment: Studio Hinrichs wanted to visually commemorate the heroes and honor the victims of the attack on September 11th, 2001.

Approach: Kit is an American Flag collector, and he recognized the proliferation of the flag following the attacks on 9/11/2001. He felt it an appropriate icon to represent the loss of so many lives. The design is distilled into two of the prominent symbols surrounding the attacks: the date and the flag. The date September 11th is itself a symbol of the resilience of a country and its people. Reinforcing the somberness of the event, the flag is printed in black on black, which stands in contrast to the brightly patriotic date.

Results: The poster has been well received by the public, design organizations, galleries, and exhibits, and it resonates with American and international audiences alike. Most recently, 9.11 has been incorporated in some nonprofit exhibits, such as Graphic Intervention.

Designer: Kit Hinrichs | **Design Firm:** Studio Hinrichs | **Client:** Studio Hinrichs

Assignment: Michael Schwab Studio was commissioned to commemorate an elegant fundraising evening for the Special Olympics in Maryland. The theme of the evening was "world travel."

Approach: My goal was to evoke the elegance and style of air travel back in the 1930s without appearing overly retro or old-fashioned. The creative director, Tom Schneidwind, suggested that I portray a Pan Am Clipper—an appropriate icon for the theme of the evening and for the elite guests. I bought a beautiful wooden model of the aircraft and photographed it in the studio from various angles. The words and image worked well together to create the desired effect.

Designer: Michael Schwab I **Design Firm:** Michael Schwab Studio I **Client:** Special Olympics Maryland

DREAMS
AND
DESTINATIONS

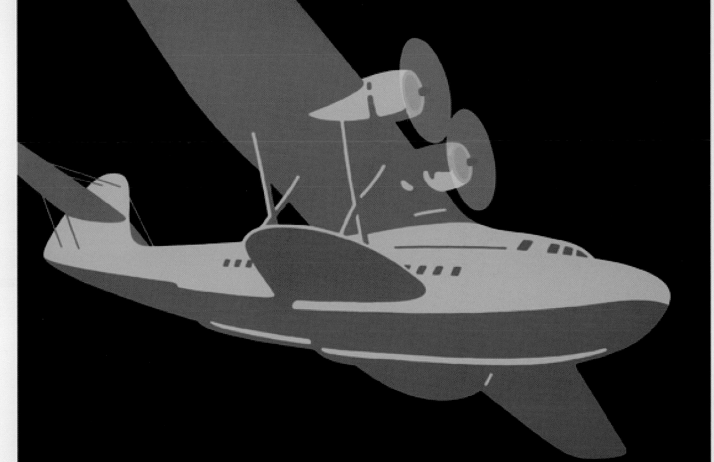

THE GLAMOUR OF
ESCAPE

Assignment: Michael Schwab Studio was commissioned to commemorate the 2013 America's Cup sailing event on San Francisco Bay, California.

Approach: I wanted to create a graphic image that evoked the beauty, power, and drama of this historic event.

My strategy was to avoid technical nautical design details and run with a "less is more" approach—typical of my graphic style.

Results: The client was very happy with the results. I received several positive and intriguing comments such as: "Looks like sharks in the water,"

"The tilted water/horizon line really feels like the viewer is in motion," "The Golden Gate Bridge is a mythical presence watching over the race."

Designer: Michael Schwab | **Design Firm:** Michael Schwab Studio | **Client:** James Whitburn, America's Cup 2013

AMERICA'S CUP

SCHWAB

SAN FRANCISCO 2013

AMERICA'S
CUP

Assignment: Blow Up is the first joint publication by photographic collective Pool, with each artist developing a new series of images specifically for the project. The task was to design a magazine that exhibited and celebrated five very different styles of photography, showcasing them as both individuals and a collective—in one harmonious publication.

Approach: The design concept is based upon incorporating the idea of a collective of artists into the physical structure of a publication. Each photographer's work is printed on a different size and paper stock, all interlocking together to form a single A1 publication; a complete, sequential magazine that then separates into five distinct books, showcasing the dissimilar perspectives and common ideals of the artistic collective. We designed the magazine to remain clean, simple, and respectful of the photographer's work, while encouraging readers to pull it apart and create their own edits. This was an extremely challenging task as any adjustment to the design of the individual books had a knock-on effect in the main magazine, as we tried to create a ceaseless flow and symmetry on each and every spread. It is a project of extraordinary invisible detail.

Designer: David Park, Richard Smalley, Ben Crick, Hampus Jageland, Mathew Hannah, Dmote
Design Firm: Maud | **Client:** Pool Photographic Collective

INTO
THE ABYSS

DISCARD

S033o 56' 40.80" E 151o 09' 31.80"

P9 / 45

WALK

DANNY
EASTWOOD

INGVÄR
KENNE

SEAN
IZZARD

CHRISTOPHER
IRELAND

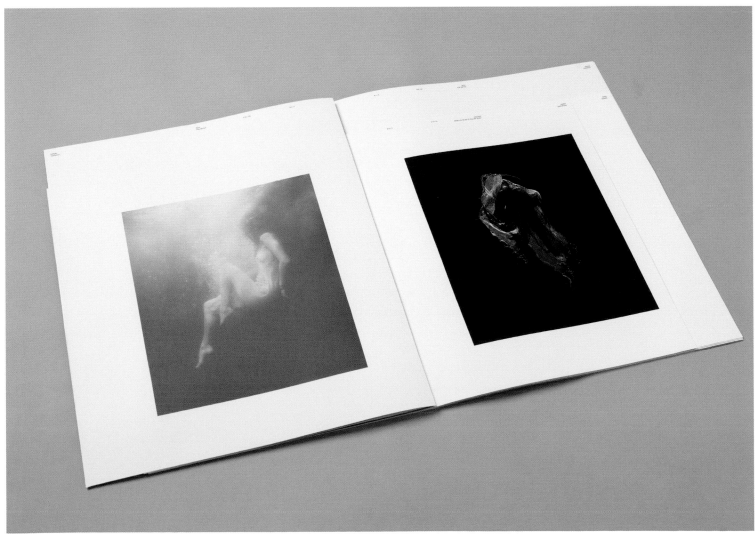

Assignment: The DIY calendar is part of our self promotion project: BITRI (a special brand of our studio that specializes in exquisite and luxurious objects all conceptualized and designed by us). This particular calendar is all about freedom and a lot of writing. It can be used as both a calendar and a diary, giving the user the freedom to give each day as many pages as he wishes. The stickers indicate the day of the month, and can be applied anywhere in the page, allowing the user to write around it.

Approach: The main objective with this project was to develop a do-it-yourself object; one that can be built differently by each person and personalized as one might desire.

Designer: Eduardo Aires | **Design Firm:** White Studio | **Client:** Bitri

YE
DIY
AR

DIARY

Assignment: Every year for the past thirty years, Webster has sent a holiday mailing to clients, friends, and colleagues to express our appreciation for their business and support. The Retro Moto served not only as the 2011/2012 holiday mailing, it is also our 30th anniversary commemorative.

Approach: The last several holiday mailings have been tin toys in custom designed packaging, which have resulted in a great deal of praise from the recipients. We decided to motor down the same path with a retro motorcycle, complete with a sidecar, symbolic of all of the wonderful surprises we have received and delivered over our thirty-year history. The package in the sidecar is actually a miniature replica of the larger package.

Results: The results have been an overwhelming amount of e-mails from tickled recipients and our Retro Moto lovingly displayed on the desks of clients and friends, from CEOs to interns, silently reminding them of their friends at Webster.

Designer: Nate Perry | **Design Firm:** Webster | **Creative Director:** Dave Webster | **Client:** Webster

Assignment: To combat the hotel's rising energy costs from cleaning and water, Hard Rock Hotel San Diego tasked MiresBall with designing a program that was accessible, memorable, and in-sync with the hotel's edgy brand.

Assignment: MiresBall developed a name, "Black is the New Green," that lent a rock & roll authenticity, while clearly explaining the sustainability program. The type-driven design highlighted the strong voice for the campaign, and the black-and-white look matched the rooms' decor and, in the case of the door hangers, also had a functional purpose: serving as an immediate flag for the cleaning staff.

Designers: Dylan Jones, Kathya Fredricks | **Design Firm:** MiresBall | **Creative Director:** Scott Mires
Copywriter: Brian Ellstrom | **Account Supervisor:** Kathy Carpentier-Moore | **Client:** Hard Rock Hotel San Diego

Assignment: At Target Headquarters, October is Design Month. 2011's theme was, "Where do ideas come from?" Our assignment was to promote various speakers and events throughout the month. A simple poster campaign was requested.

Approach: The creative process went like this: 1) procrastinate, 2) walk to coffee shop, 3) bounce ideas around, 4) arrive at the epiphany: let's answer the question, "where do ideas come from?" with a one-word answer: HERE. Meaning, everywhere. Which is exactly where these elements lived. (There were other ideas, but the "HERE" campaign was the only idea enthusiastically sold—and, as we'd hoped, it was enthusiastically chosen by the client. So enthusiastically, in fact, the poster request grew into a much larger campaign.)

Results: Every event and speaker session was well-attended. Target team members embraced the campaign, got guerrilla and stuck the "Here" stickers all over the corporate offices (and the surrounding concrete jungle) in downtown Minneapolis, creating a yellow movement in an otherwise red, white, and round environment.

Designer: David Schwen | **Design Firm:** Target inHouse | **Client:** Target

Where do ideas come from?

Assignment: Keaykolour is a paper range manufactured by ArjoWiggins Creative Papers (UK). Keaykolour is available in a range of colors, weights, and finishes. We were commissioned to create a promotion for the Australian market that demonstrated the creative possibilities of the paper.

Approach: We set out to create something of a keepsake, that would stand out from so many paper promotions that end up in the bottom of the samples drawer. Our solution was a set of alphabet "flash" cards bound together with a rubber band. We conveyed the versatility of the paper through expressive typography and a range of different printing effects and embellishments.

Designers: Paul Garbett, Elise Santangelo | **Design Firm:** Naughtyfish | **Client:** ArjoWiggins

Assignment: The poster is part of the initial rebranding of Henry+Co, together with their business card that has the same embossed seal.

Approach: Once we had created their logotype and seal we incorporated both elements into the promotional poster to showcase their craftsmanship and a few of the finishing treatments they offer. Typography was picked up from their business card to ensure brand consistency, and the circle pattern reflects the back of the die-cuts they use.

Results: Henry+Co has received a number of inquiries and new jobs resulting from the new branding pieces, including this poster, and have been awarded a number of various design awards and been the subject of blog posts. The client seems rather happy.

Designer: Lionel Ferreira | **Design Firm:** Ferreira Design Company | **Client:** Henry+Co

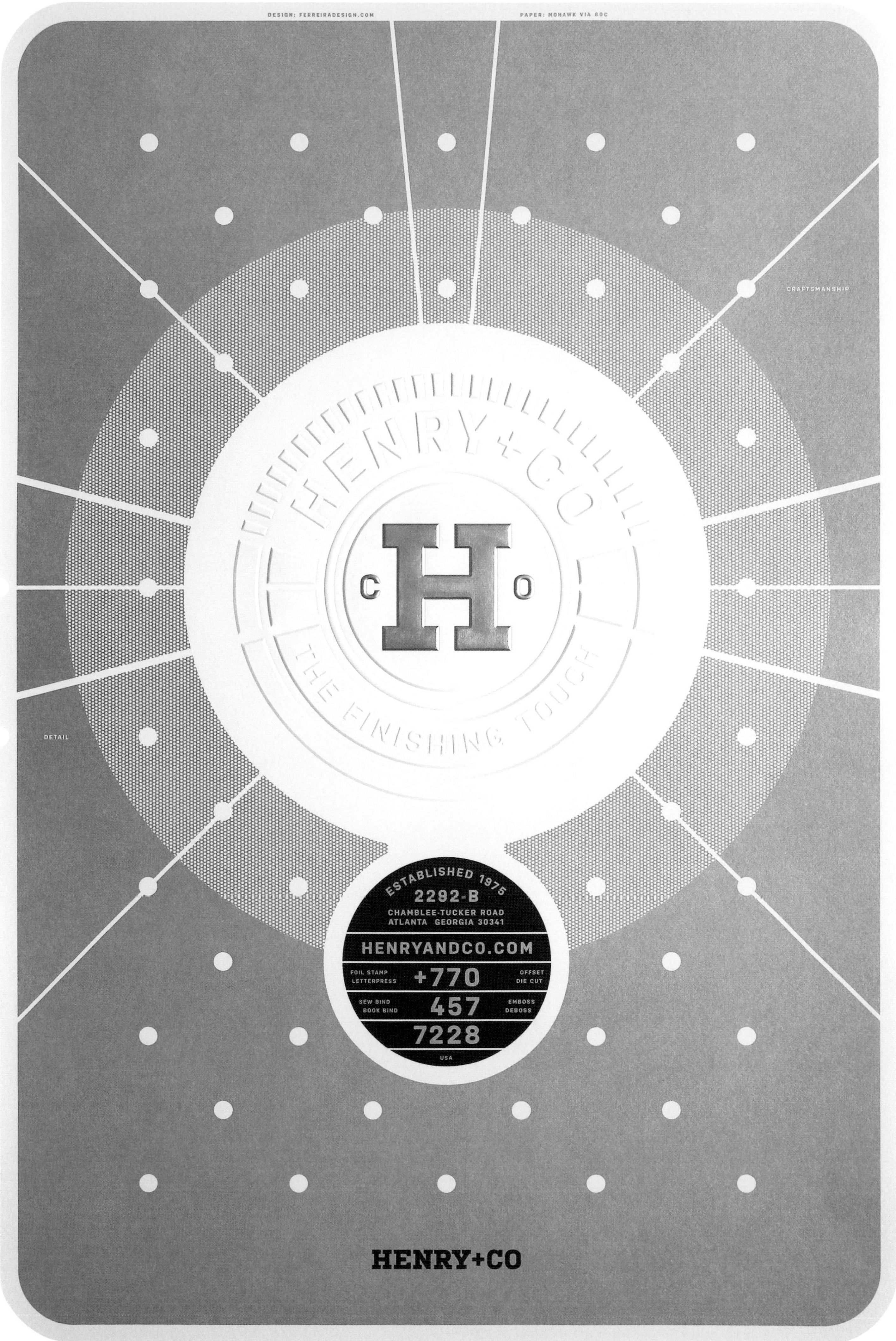

DESIGN: FERREIRADESIGN.COM   PAPER: MOHAWK VIA 80C

HENRY+CO

CRAFTSMANSHIP

HENRY+CO

THE FINISHING TOUCH

H
C   O

DETAIL

ESTABLISHED 1975
2292-B
CHAMBLEE-TUCKER ROAD
ATLANTA GEORGIA 30341

HENRYANDCO.COM

FOIL STAMP LETTERPRESS	+770	OFFSET DIE CUT
SEW BIND BOOK BIND	457	EMBOSS DEBOSS
	7228	

USA

HENRY+CO

Assignment: Bookkeeping is an industry that thrives on lining up, fitting in, and filing away. Sandra Haniak, a bookkeeper who specializes in working with small businesses, needed to stand out a little bit.

Approach: Small business. Business card. Small business card.

Results: At a compact 1.0 x 0.6 inches and letterpress printed on 220 lb. paper, these business cards are making quite the impression. Now, to find that application for the *Guinness Book of World Records*.

Designer: Hans Thiessen | **Design Firm:** WAX | **Design Director:** Monique Gamache | **Creative Director:** Joe Hospodarec
Printing: Studio on Fire | **Client:** Sandra Haniak

BOOKKEEPING FOR
SMALL BUSINESS

Assignment: This edition of *The Standard*, created for Sappi Fine Papers, is number five in a series of educational brochures that highlight specific uses of paper within the design profession. This "Special Effects" edition demonstrates many of the hundreds of different printing techniques utilized to make print communications more effective. Created in conjunction with 826 National, a non-profit organization that provides writing and tutoring services for children, the major themes of the book relate to 826's unique retail location across the country. Each of the eight centers is also home to a storefront, such as the Pirate Store, the Brooklyn Superhero Supply Co., and the Bigfoot Research Institute.

Approach: We created this piece to tell the story of special effects through the eight individual chapters of 826 National. The special techniques were paired with specific illustrators whose illustrative or photographic approach lent itself to a print technique. For example, we paired thermography with a scratchboard pirate portrait, and holographic die-stamping with illustrations of robots.

Results: Sappi felt so positively about the results of the piece, the client planned a ten-city tour, all with sold-out venues, to promote it. The Standard 5 is currently being used as an effective reference tool by designers across the country.

Designers: Kit Hinrichs, Belle Chock | **Design Firm:** Studio Hinrichs | **Client:** Sappi Fine Papers

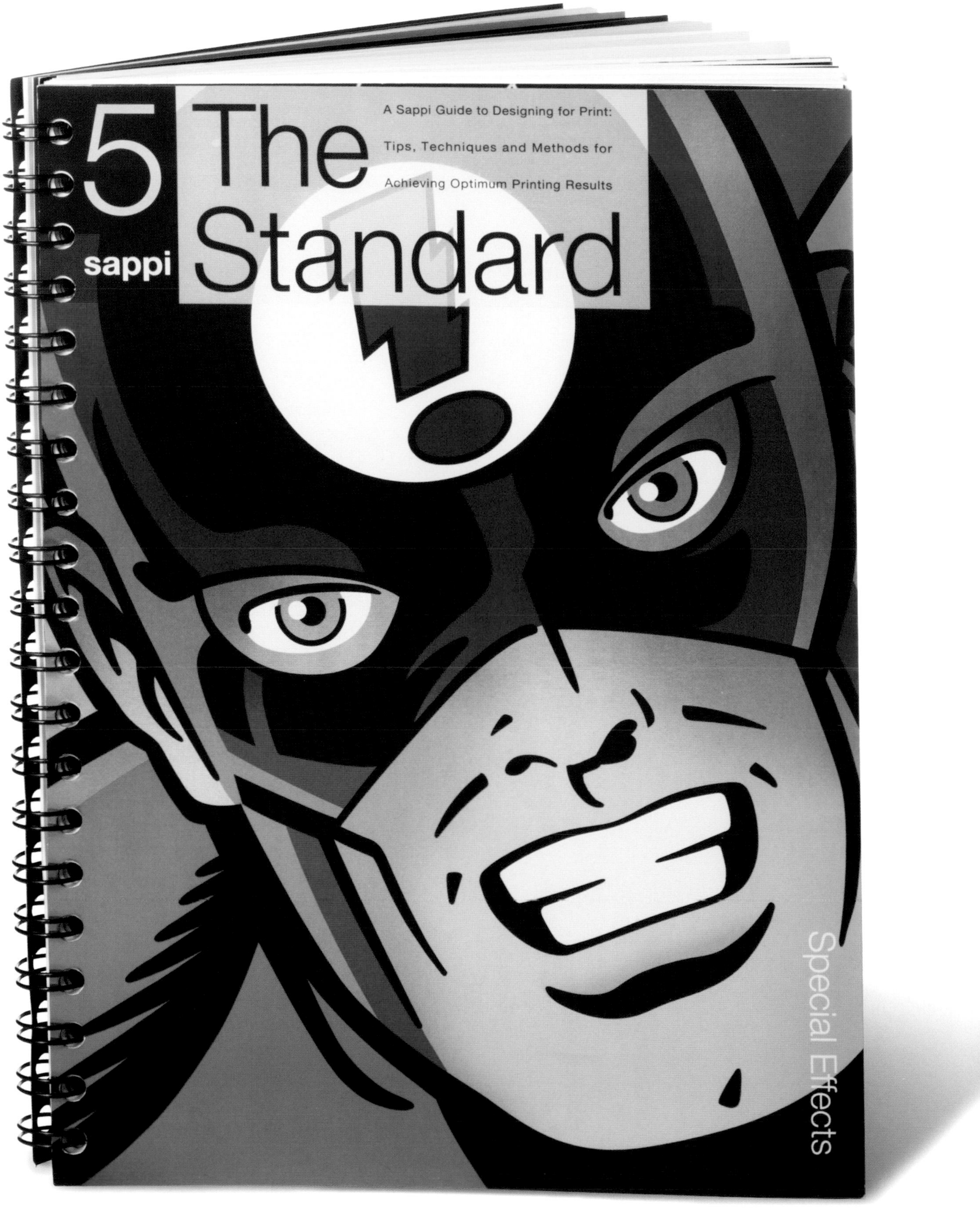

5

sappi **The Standard**

A Sappi Guide to Designing for Print:

Tips, Techniques and Methods for

Achieving Optimum Printing Results

Special Effects

Museum of Unnatural History of Washington, D.C.

Some objects found by early explorers are too weird for the nearby Smithsonian Museum of Natural History to display. Unnaturalists find the Museum of Unnatural History's collection of animals amazingly unbelievable, especially the weagle, owlephant and prehistoric skeleton of a creature that perplexes even the experts. The Museum store offers a diverse collection of impossible-to-find merchandise as well. Sabertooth dental floss, Existentially Distraught Wood, Unicorn Tears, Wallace's Primordial Soup, Future Mold, and a Field Journal (toilet paper roll that doubles as writing paper "for when you have to go write now") are all for sale in the Unnatural History's gift shop.

Captain Ahab feared the ferocious Giant Sea Bass more than he did Moby Dick the whale. Here, the ship-eating Sea Bass is engraved in blue.

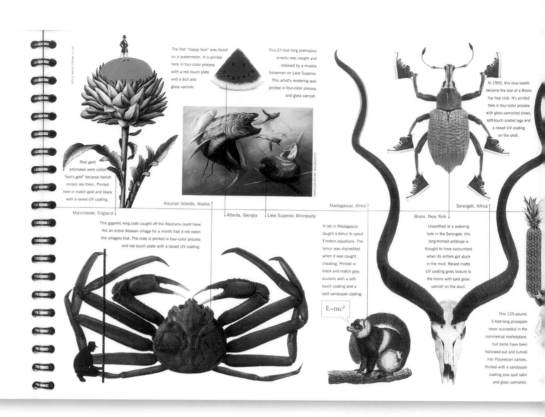

Real gold artichokes were called "fool's gold" because foolish miners ate them. Printed here in match gold and black with a raised UV coating.

Manchester, England

The first "happy face" was found on a watermelon. It is printed here in four-color process with a red touch plate and a dull and gloss varnish.

Atlanta, Georgia

This 27-foot-long prehistoric vinactu was caught and released by a muskie fisherman on Lake Superior. This artist's rendering was printed in four-color process and gloss varnish.

Lake Superior, Minnesota

Aleutian Islands, Alaska

This gigantic king crab caught off the Aleutians could have fed an entire Alaskan village for a month had it not eaten the villagers first. The crab is printed in four-color process and red touch plate with a raised UV coating.

A lab in Madagascar taught a lemur to spout Einstein equations. The lemur was discredited when it was caught cheating. Printed in black and match gray duotone with a soft-touch coating and a spot sandpaper coating.

Madagascar, Africa

$E=mc^2$

In 1992, this blue beetle became the star of a Bronx hip hop club. It's printed here in four-color process with gloss-varnished shoes, soft-touch coated legs and a raised UV coating on the shell.

Bronx, New York

Unearthed at a watering hole in the Serengeti, this long-horned antelope is thought to have succumbed when its antlers got stuck in the mud. Raised matte UV coating gives texture to the horns with spot gloss varnish on the skull.

Serengeti, Africa

This 125-pound, 5-foot-long pineapple never succeeded in the commercial marketplace, but some have been hollowed out and turned into Polynesian canoes. Printed with a sandpaper coating plus spot satin and gloss varnishes.

Special Effects. Volume 5 of The Standard shows designers how the creative use of special effects can make a printed piece dimensional, tactile, intriguing and sometimes interactive. The techniques shown here may look like magic, but many are easy for designers to prepare and can be done inline on a conventional press. All it takes are a few printing tips, the right paper, and letting your imagination go. **The Standard** from Sappi is an educational reference piece that combines the technical with the creative. This edition of The Standard is printed on McCoy, an environmentally responsive premium coated sheet renowned for its bright whiteness and unsurpassed printability. **Sappi North America** is also the maker of top-selling coated brands—Opus, Somerset and Flo.

This giant broad-winged bat was hunted to extinction by umbrella makers. Printed in black and match gray with a raised matte UV coating.

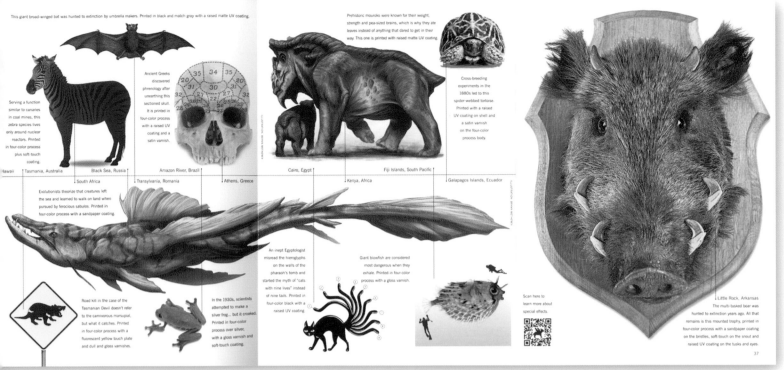

Serving a function similar to canaries in coal mines, this zebra species lives only around nuclear reactors. Printed in four-color process plus soft-touch coating.

Ancient Greeks discovered phrenology after unearthing this sectioned skull. It is printed in four-color process with a raised UV coating and a satin varnish.

Prehistoric mouroks were known for their weight, strength and pea-sized brains, which is why they ate leaves instead of anything that dared to get in their way. This one is printed with raised matte UV coating.

Cross-breeding experiments in the 1880s led to this spider-webbed tortoise. Printed with a raised UV coating on shell and a satin varnish on the four-color process body.

Hawaii | Tasmania, Australia | Black Sea, Russia | Amazon River, Brazil | Athens, Greece | Cairo, Egypt | Kenya, Africa | Galapagos Islands, Ecuador

South Africa | Transylvania, Romania

Evolutionists theorize that creatures left the sea and learned to walk on land when pursued by ferocious sabulos. Printed in four-color process with a sandpaper coating.

Road kill in the case of the Tasmanian Devil doesn't refer to the carnivorous marsupial, but what it catches. Printed in four-color process with a fluorescent yellow touch plate and dull and gloss varnishes.

In the 1930s, scientists attempted to make a silver frog... but it croaked. Printed in four-color process over silver, with a gloss varnish and soft-touch coating.

An inept Egyptologist misread the hieroglyphs on the walls of the pharaoh's tomb and started the myth of "cats with nine lives" instead of nine tails. Printed in four-color black with a raised UV coating.

Giant blowfish are considered most dangerous when they exhale. Printed in four-color process with a gloss varnish.

Scan here to learn more about special effects.

Little Rock, Arkansas — The multi-tusked boar was hunted to extinction years ago. All that remains is this mounted trophy, printed in four-color process with a sandpaper coating on the bristles, soft-touch on the snout and raised UV coating on the tusks and eyes.

The Brooklyn Superhero Supply Co.

Disguise wearing thin? Capes in a choice of colors can be found at the Superhero Supply Co., along with a wind chamber to test if it can get airborne. The store also sells its own private-label brand of Speed of Light in liquid form, Gravity by the gallon and Evil Blob Containment Capsule in 10-ounce size, enough to get superheroes by in a pinch. The secret identity kits and suction cups are the best in Brooklyn and antimatter is offered at unbeatable prices. With the economy in the doldrums, the Superhero Supply Co. has also introduced a Sidekick Placement Service for superhero assistants looking for work.

More powerful than uranium, this chunk of "kryptonite" glows with energy, thanks to a black and brown duotone and touch plates of silver and green inks. A gloss varnish covers the green, with a sandpaper finish on the rest of the rock.

PHOTOGRAPH: TERRY HEFFERNAN

Superwoman bursts out of the "torn" pages of comic books. Created as a single illustration made to appear like torn panels drawn in different styles, the pop culture image is printed in four-color process, with each panel delineated by ink substitutions and touch plates that included fluorescent inks, match colors and metallics.

ILLUSTRATION: LOU BROOKS

This robot was die-stamped with special foil stamps—holographic and brushed aluminum. The foils were applied with two passes through the press. The black and four-color process were printed on a separate pass.

Scan here to learn more about special effects.

ILLUSTRATION: PATRICK HRUBY

GETTY IMAGES

Scratchboard, an art technique that originated in the 19th century, seemed right for when pirates roamed the Seven Seas. The textural quality of scratchboard was simulated with thermography, a heat-set, raised ink printing technique. The proximity of the pirate's gold tooth and copper earring on the artwork allowed two foil strips to be applied in a single pass on press.

ILLUSTRATION: BILL SANDERSON

The tactile smoothness of glass and the dimensional outline of a bottle were suggested by applying a raised gloss UV coating over the bottle area. The image itself was printed in four-color process with a match gray and spot varnish.

IMAGINATION IS A LIMITLESS PLACE, FREE OF BOUNDARIES AND FILLED WITH POSSIBILITIES. IT WELCOMES ALL IDEAS, PRACTICAL AND FANTASTIC, SIMPLE AND COMPLEX, INVENTIVE AND MUNDANE, ALLOWING THEM TO EXIST UNJUDGED IN THE SAME TIME AND SPACE WITHOUT A SECOND THOUGHT. IMAGINATION INSPIRES CREATIVITY, NURTURING THE FIRST INKLING OF AN IDEA UNTIL IT EMERGES FULLY FORMED AND READY TO TAKE FLIGHT.

Assignment: The School of Visual Arts has been creating posters for New York City subway platforms for decades. The posters are familiar to all straphangers and have become a part of the culture of NYC. SVA's goal is to continually commission new artists and designers to create something unique that will bring attention to the school and its excellence.

Approach: This year's poster was created by Steven Heller and Viktor Koen. In Heller's own words, "There is no better way to get across SVA's three common themes—Art (which includes design), Business (which includes entrepreneurship), and Culture (which is the entire ball of wax)—than through Koen's ABeCeDarian."

Designers: Steven Heller, Viktor Koen | **Design Firm:** Visual Arts Press, Ltd. | **Client:** School of Visual Arts

the *ABCs* of SVA
ART · BUSINESS · CULTURE

www.sva.edu School of VISUAL ARTS®

art direction: Steven Heller · design & illustration: Viktor Koen

CANADA

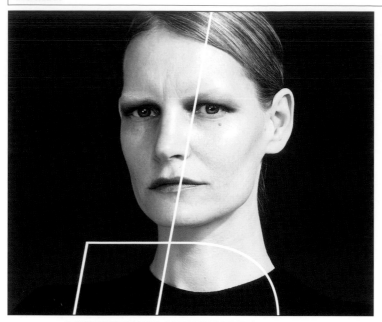

CONCRETE DESIGN COMMUNICATIONS | Lida Baday

UNDERLINE STUDIO | Prefix Photo

BRAZIL

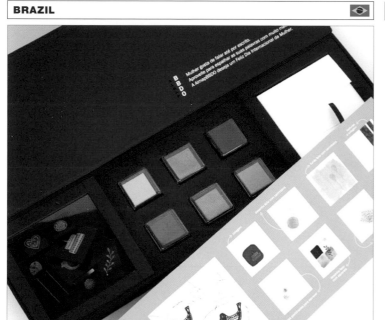

SUPERBACANA DESIGN | Almap BBDO

MEXICO

PARALELO | Fuga Chocolate Store

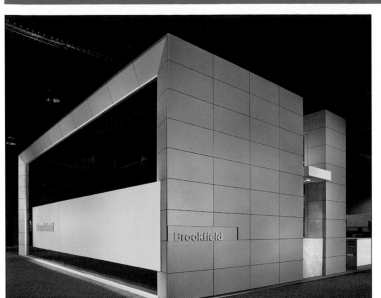

JAN LORENC, CHUNG YOUL YOO, STEWART SONDERMAN | Georgia

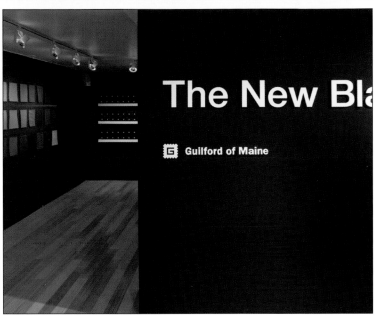

YANG KIM | Peopledesign | Michigan

KATE ARENDS, PAUL SIEKA | **Brown-Forman** | Minnesota

NATE PERRY | Webster | Nebraska

KATE ARENDS | **Brown-Forman** | Minnesota

LIONEL FERREIRA | Henry+Co | Georgia

KIT HINRICHS | Studio Hinrichs

BUTLER LOONEY | The Coca-Cola Company North America

MICHAEL VANDERBYL, PETER FISHEL, DAVID HARD | Luna Textiles

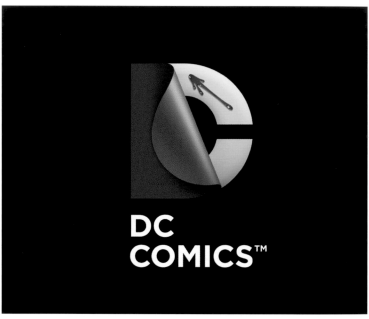

MICHAEL LIN, MARTIN KOVAKOVSKY, JESSICA MINN | DC Comincs

JACQUELINE NORHEIM | Erica Tanov

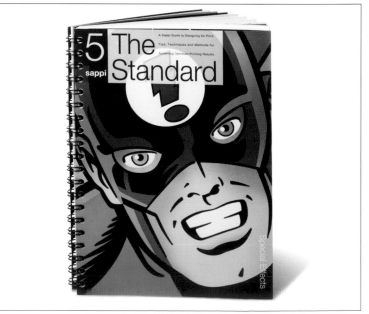

KIT HINRCHS, BELLE CHOCK | Sappi Fine Papers

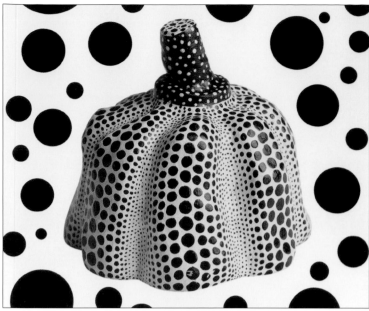

TIRSO MONTAN, CHRISTINA FREYSS | Sotheby's

GLENN CHAN | SL Green Realty Corp.

JOHN PASSAFIUME, DANA TANAMACHI | School of Visual Arts

DOUG LLOYD, ASAKO AEBA | Tom Ford

BENJAMIN BOURS | GQ Magazine

JOE SHOULDICE | Vilcek Foundation

CANADA

ClubLink	entro | G+A	FYC	Paprika	The White Room Inc
Coastlines Creative Group	Forge Media + Design	lg2boutique	Sasges Inc.	Underline Studio
Concrete Design	Foundry	MacLaren McCann Calgary	Steiner Graphics	WAX

USA

14-Forty	Cue	GQ Magazine	Lightner Design	Palio	stollerbarakatdesign
160over90	DAAKE	Greenfield/Belser	Lippincott	Paragon Design International, Inc.	Stoltze Design
21xdesign	DarbyDarbyCreative	GSD&M	Little & Company		Studio 32 North
9Threads	David Sutherland Inc	Guy Villa Design	little fish studio	Pennebaker	Studio Hinrichs
Addison	Decker Design	gyro	LLOYD&CO	Pentagram	Studio Scott
Afloat Studios	Design is Play	hawkeye	Lorenc+Yoo Design	People Design	Tactical Magic
ALCHEMY LTD	Dragon Rouge	Hello Design	Los Angeles County Museum of Art	Peppermill Projects	Target Corporation
American Committee for the Weizmann Institute of Science	Drew Allison	Hint Creative		Peter Mayer Advertising	TBWA Chiat Day
	Ellen Bruss Design	HOOK	Mark Oliver, Inc.	Peterson Ray & Company	The Art Institute of Houston
	EMdash Design	Hub Strategy	Matsumoto Inc.	PorchCreative	The Richards Group
And Partners Ny	Emerson, Wajdowicz Studios	IF Studio	McGraw-Hill Construction	Projekt, Inc.	TOKY Branding + Design
Bailey Lauerman		Innocean Worldwide Americas	McMillan Group	Publications & Graphics	Trinity Brand Group
Baldwin & Lyons, Inc.	Esparza Advertising		meter industries	Ralph Appelbaum Ass, Inc.	TRUF
Barker Design, Inc.	Faine/Oller Productions, Inc.	Jay Advertising	Method, Inc.	RBMM	Turner Duckworth
BEING	Ferreira Design Company	Joe Shouldice	Methodologie	Sagon-Phior	Vanderbyl Design
BEING	Fleishman-Hillard	John McNeil Studio	Michael Schwab Studio	San Francisco AIDS Foundation	Visual Arts Press, Ltd.
Better Than One	G2	Jovenville	mindsalt		Volume Inc.
BradfordLawton	GCF, Inc	Karim Rashid	Minelli, Inc	Savage	Wallace Church, Inc.
CH Design	Gee + Chung Design	ken-tsai lee design studio	MiresBall	Schatz Ornstein Studio	Webster
Colle + McVoy	Gemineye Studio	Kiyoshi TOGASHI Klim Design, Inc.	Morla Design	SF Weekly	Weymouth Design
Column Five Media	Goodby, Silverstein & Partners		MRM/McCann	SHR Perceptual Branding	White & Case LLP
Concussion LLP	Goodby, Silverstein & Partners	Kym Abrams Design	Nesnadny + Schwartz	Skaarva Design	YARD
Conservation Services		Landor Associates	Odgis + Company	Sotheby's	
Craig-Teerlink Design		Let There Be Dragons	Ostro Design	Sterling Cross Creative	

MEXICO

paralelo 19

BRAZIL

superbacana design

ITALY

TW2 | Davide Cenci

ANDREA CASTELLETTI | Help Japan

PORTUGAL

WHITE STUDIO | BITRI

WHITE STUDIO | Esporão

FINLAND

Laura Suuronen

GERMANY

beierarbeit GmbH	Delikatessen Agentur fÃ¼r	hÃ¤felinger+wagner design	KMS TEAM GmbH	Studio Tomeczek
Claus Koch GmbH	Marken und Design GmbH	gmbh	Lattke und Lattke	

ICELAND

Leynivopnid	Thorleifur Gunnar Gislason

ITALY

Andrea Castelletti	H-57 Creative Station	Raineri Design Srl	TW2

NETHERLANDS

Total Public

NORWAY

StrÃ¸mme Throndsen Design

PORTUGAL

AnaMoreira	AntÃ³nio Queiros Design	White Studio

ROMANIA

Brandient	Synopsis

SLOVENIA

design center ltd.

SPAIN

Bisgrafic	Unlimited Creative Group

SWITZERLAND

Gottschalk+Ash Int'l

UK

Appetite London	Christie's	Consultants	Exposed Design	oakwood media group
ArthurSteenHorneAdamson	Clarus	DMWORKROOM	Neuronalics Ltd.	Springetts Brand Design

NORWAY

STRØMME THRONDSEN DESIGN | Jens Eide

ITALY

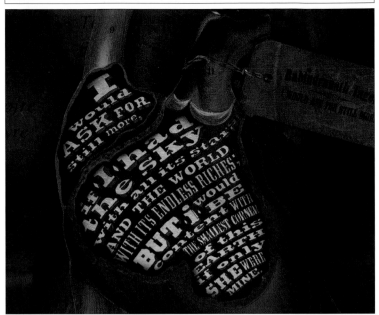

H-57 CREATIVE STATION | FirstFloorUnder.com

GERMANY

FEBRÜ | Febrü Corporate Design

PORTUGAL

ANTONIO QUEIROS DESIGN | Monte da Raposinha

SPAIN

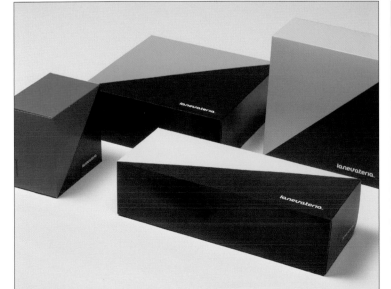

BISGRÀFIC | La Nevateria

UNITED KINGDOM

OAKWOOD MEDIA GROUP | Air BP Lubricants

REPUBLIC OF KOREA

DANKOOK UNIVERSITY | Hoondong Chung

JAPAN

OMDR DESIGN AGENCY | Akane Saito

AUSTRALIA

PEEL DESIGN | Pacific Brands Underwear Group

FROST DESIGN | Manfredi Enterprise

AUSTRALIA

Blow.	Frost design	Hoyne	Naughtyfish design	Peel Design	Watts Design
Boccalatte	Housemouse	Maud	Next brand futures pty ltd	SML / Small Medium Large	

CHINA

Beamy Creative

JAPAN

Good morning inc.	Graphic communication	laboratory	Ogawayouhei Design Desk	Omdr design agency

KOREA

Dankook University

NEW ZEALAND

Alt Group

SINGAPORE

Epigram

TURKEY

GRAFFITI	Atelo	BEK Design	Springetts Brand Design

WINNERS DIRECTORY

160over90 www.160over90.com
1 South Broad
Philadelphia, PA 19107, United States
Tel 215-732-3200 | Fax 215-732-1664

A Green Hill Communications Limited
803 8/F Park, Commercial Ctr. 180
Tung Lo Wan Rd., Hong Kong
Tel +852 2508 9196

Addison Design Co. www.addison.com
20 Exchange Place, Ste. 9
New York, NY 10005, United States
Tel 212-229-5000

Alt Group www.altgroup.net
16-18 Mackelvie Street, Grey Lynn
PO Box 47873
Ponsonby 1144
Auckland, New Zealand
Tel +64 9 360 3910

Andrea Castelletti Design / TW2
http://daltraparte.prosite.com
Via Breno 2
20139, Milan, Italy
Tel +39 02 87 39 16 84

António Queirós Design
Avenida Da Boavista, 3521 – Salas 603/604
4100-139 Porto, Portugal
Tel 35 1 226 169 717 | Fax 35 1 226 169 719

ArthurSteenHorneAdamson
www.ashawebsite.co.uk
Suite 404, Eagle Tower,
Montpellier Drive
Cheltenham, Gloucestershire
GL50 1TA, United Kingdom
Tel +44 12 4257 4111

Bisgràfic www.bisgrafic.com
Avinguda del Mercat 8, 4th Floor
Vic, Barcelona 8500, Spain
Tel 93 883 59 80 | Fax 93 889 55 12

Bradford Lawton www.bradfordlawton.com
1020 Townsend Ave.
San Antonio, TX 78209, United States
Tel 210-832-0555

Colle + McVoy
400 First Ave. North, Suite 700
Minneapolis, MN 55401, United States
Tel 612-305-6000 | Fax 612-305-6500

Concrete Design Communications
2 Silver Avenue, 2nd Floor
Toronto, Ontario M6R 3A2, Canada
Tel 416-534-9960 | Fax 416-534-2184

Cue http://designcue.com
520 Nicollet Mall, Suite 500
Minneapolis, MN 55402, United States
Tel 612-465-0030

Dankook University
www.so-nu.info/Dankook-College-of-Arts
126, Jukjeon-dong, Suji-gu,
Dankook University, College of Art,
Dept. of Visual Communication Design, Room 317
Gyeonggi-do 448-701, Republic of Korea
Tel 031 8005 3083

David Sutherland Inc. deckerdesign.com
679 Danielle Ct.
Rockwall, TX 75087,
United States
Tel 972 771 0680

Decker Design deckerdesign.com
14 West 23rd Street, 3rd Floor
New York, NY 10010, United States
Tel 212-633-8588

Design is Play www.designisplay.com
855 Folsom Street, No. 931
San Francisco, CA 94107, United States
Tel 415-505-6242

Drew Allison: Brand Expression
www.drew-allison.com
4 Orchard St.
Watertown, MA 02472, United States
Tel 617-926-6478

entro | G+A www.entro.com
122 Parliament Street
Toronto, ON M5A 2Y8, Canada
Tel 416-368-6988 | Fax 416-368-5616

Febrü www.februe.de
Im Babenbecker
Feld 62
32051 Herford, Germany
Tel +49 (0) 5221 3804-0 | Fax +49 (0) 5221 3804-29

Ferreira Design Company
www.ferreiradesign.com
335 Stevens Creek Court
Alpharetta, GA 30005, United States
Tel 678-297-1903

Foundry foundrycommunications.ca
301, 221 10th Ave. SE
Calgary AB T2G0V9, Canada
Tel 403-237-8084

frost* design www.frostdesign.com.au
Level 1, 15 Foster Street, Surry Hills
Sydney, Australia
Tel +61 2 9280 42 33

Gee + Chung Design www.geechungdesign.com
38 Bryant Street, Suite 100
San Francisco, CA 94105, United States
Tel 415-543-1192

Goodby, Silverstein & Partners
www.greenfieldbelser.com
720 California Street
San Francisco, CA 94108, United States
Tel 415-955-5683

GQ Magazine www.gq.com
4 Times Square, 9th Floor
New York, NY 10036, United States
Tel 212-286-6695

Greenfield/Belser www.greenfieldbelser.com
1818 N Street NW, Suite 110
Washington DC 20036, United States
Tel 202-775-0333 | Fax 202-775-0402

H-57 Creative Station www.h-57.com
via Washington 72
20146 Milan, Italy
Tel/Fax +39 02 36 68 58 81

Henry & Co. www.hookusa.com
2292-B Chamblee Tucker Road
Chamblee, GA 30341
Tel 770-457-7228

HOOK www.hookusa.com
409 King Street, Floor 4
Charleston, SC 29403, United States
Tel 843-853-5532

IF Studio www.ifstudiony.com
670 Broadway, Suite 301
New York, NY 10012, United States
Tel 212-334-3465

John McNeil Studio johnmcneilstudio.com
720 Channing Street
Berkeley, CA 94710, United States
Tel 510-526-7100

ken-tsai lee design studio
99-44 62nd Road, Rego Park
New York, NY 11374, United States
Tel 718-592-9152

Klim Design, Inc. www.klimdesign.com
P.O. Box Y
Avon, CT 6001 United States
Tel 860-678-1222

Landor Associates landor.com
1001 Front Street
San Francisco, CA 94111, United States
Tel 415-365-3713

Lippincott www.lippincott.com
499 Park Avenue
New York, NY 10022, United States
Tel 212-521-0054

LLOYD&CO www.lloydandco.com
180 Varick Street, Suite 1018
New York, NY 10014, United States
Tel 212-414-3100 | Fax 212-414-3113

**Lorenc+Yoo Design & Journey
Communications, Inc.** www.lorencyoodesign.com
109 Vickery Street
Roswell, GA 30075, United States
Tel 770-645-2828 | Fax 770-998-2452

Louise Fili, Ltd. www.louisefili.com
310 East 23rd Street, Suite 8F
New York, NY 10010
Tel 212-989-9153

Maud www.maud.com.au
Ground Suit 5, 59 Great Buckingham St.
Redfern, New South Wales 2016, Australia
Tel +61 (0)2 8665 4257

Michael Schwab Studio www.michaelschwab.com
108 Tamalpais Avenue
San Anselmo, CA 94960, United States
Tel 415-257-5792 | Fax 415-257-5793

MiresBall www.miresball.com
2605 State St.
San Diego, CA 92103, United States
Tel 619-234-6631

Naughtyfish design www.naughtyfish.com.au
Suite 306b, 19a Boundary Street
Rushcutters Bay, NSW 2011, Australia
Tel +612 9357 5911

omdr design agency www.omdr.co.jp
107-0062 Unity 6-12-10 Minami-Aoyama
Minato-ku, Tokyo 202, Japan
Tel 03-5766-3410 | Fax 03-5766-3411

OMG (Oakwood Media Group)
www.oakwood-mg.com
Creative Studio
7 Park Street
Bristol BS1 5NF, United Kingdom
Tel +44 (0) 117 983 6789

Peel Design www.peel-design.com.au
715 Rathdowne Street
Carlton North, Melbourne, Australia
Tel +61 3 9349 2149

People Design peopledesign.com
648 Monroe NW, Suite 212
Grand Rapids, MI 49503, United States
Tel 616-459-4444

Peter Mayer Advertising www.peteramayer.com
318 Camp Street
New Orleans, LA 70130, United States
Tel 504-581-7191 | Fax 504-566-1046

Ph.D. A Design Office http://phdla.com
1702 Olympic Blvd.
Santa Monica, CA 90404
Tel 310-452-8200

Ralph Appelbaum Associates Inc. www.raany.com
88 Pine Street, 29th Floor
New York, NY 10005, United States
Tel 212-334-8200 | Fax 212-334-6214

Schatz Ornstein Studio www.howardschatz.com
435 West Broadway, 2nd Floor
New York, NY 11211, United States
Tel 212-334-6667 | Fax 212-334-6669

SML / Small Medium Large
www.smallmediumlarge.com.au
412 / 2-4 Powell Street
Waterloo NSW 2017, Australia
Tel 62296999709

Sotheby's www.sothebys.com/en.html
1334 York Avenue
New York, NY 10021, United States
Tel 212-894-1180

Strømme Throndsen Design
www.smallmediumlarge.com.au
Holtegaten 22 Oslo
Oslo 355 Norway
Tel 4722963900

Studio 32 North studio32north.com
3315 Thorn Street
San Diego, CA 92104, United States
Tel 619-546-9343

Studio Hinrichs www.studio-hinrichs.com
368 Clementina Street
San Francisco, CA 94103, United States
Tel 415-543-1776 | Fax 415-543-1775

Superbacana Design
superbacana@superbacanadesign.com.br
av. brig. faria lima, 2012 6° andar
cep 01451 000
são paulo sp brasil
Tel 55 11 3815 8429 | Fax 55 11 3817 4742

Target www.target.com
33 South Sixth Street CC-03
Minneapolis, MN 55402, United States
Tel 612-304-9858

The White Room Inc.
Design/Art Direction
www.thewhiteroom.ca
191 First Avenue
Toronto, ON M4M 1X3, Canada
Tel 416-901-7736

TOKY Branding + Design www.toky.com
3001 Locust St.
St. Louis, MO 63103, United States
Tel 314-534-2000

Turner Duckworth www.turnerduckworth.com
831 Montgomery Street
San Francisco, CA 94133, United States
Tel 415-675-7777

Underline Studio www.underlinestudio.com
247 Wallace Avenue, 2nd Floor
Toronto, ON M6H 1V5, Canada
Tel 416-341-0475

Vanderbyl Design www.vanderbyldesign.com
171 2ND Street, 2nd Floor
San Francisco, CA 94105, United States
Tel 415-543-8447 | Fax 415-543-9058

Visual Arts Press, Ltd.
220 East 23rd Street, Suite 311
New York, NY 10010, United States
Tel 212-592-2380

WAX www.wax.ca
320 333 24th Ave. SW
Calgary AB T2S 3E6, Canada
Tel 403-262-9323

Webster Design Associates
www.websterdesign.com
5060 Dodge Street, Suite 2000
Omaha, NE 68132, United States
Tel 402-551-0503

White Studio www.whitestudio.pt
Rua da Cerca, no5
Porto 4150-202, Portugal
Tel +351 226 169 080

YARD www.yardnyc.com
130 W. 25th St., 7th Floor
New York, NY 10001, United States
Tel 212-625-8372 | Fax 212-625-1460

YesYesYes Design http://yesyesyes.es/
112 Second Avenue, Studio 30
Brooklyn, NY 11215, United States
Tel 718-501-4995

DESIGNERS

ART DIRECTORS / CREATIVE DIRECTORS

DESIGN FIRMS

PHOTOGRAPHERS

COPYWRITERS

CLIENTS

How to save on our Graphis Books

Standing Orders:

50% off or $60 for a $120 book, plus $10 for shipping & handling
Get our new books at our best deal, long before they arrive in book
stores! A Standing Order is a subscription commiment to the Graphis
books of your choice.

How to save on our Graphis Books

Standing Orders:
50% off or $60 for a $120 book, plus $10 for shipping & handling
Get our new books at our best deal, long before they arrive in book
stores! A Standing Order is a subscription commiment to the Graphis
books of your choice.

Graphis Titles

Poster Annual 2013

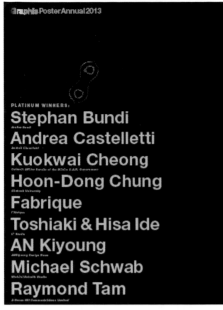

2013
Hardcover: 240 pages
200-plus color illustrations

Trim: 8.5 x 11.75"
ISBN: 1-931241-29-8
US $120

Graphis Poster 2013 is the definitive showcase of the 100 best Posters of the year chosen from numerous international entries. The collection features 9 Platinum and 91 Gold award-winning Posters from Italy, South Africa, Switzerland, Korea, The Netherlands, Japan and the United States, amongst many others. Graphis also features an interview with **Rick Valicenti**, the founder and Design Director of Thirst in Chicago — a firm devoted to "art, function and real human presence."

Advertising Annual 2013

2013
Hardcover: 256 pages
200-plus color images

Trim: 7 x 11 3/4"
ISBN: 1-932026-79-5
US $120

Graphis Advertising 2013 presents some of the top campaigns of the year selected from hundreds of entries. Featured are seasoned works from accomplished advertising agencies, such as **Goodby, Silverstein & Partners**, **Bailey Lauerman**, **BVK**, **DeVito/Verdi**, **HOOK**, and **Saatchi & Saatchi**. Each spread presents the work with a case study description written by each agency. These campaigns provide insight into the agency's creative process and how they met the needs of their clients.

Design Annual 2013

2013
Hardcover: 256 pages
200-plus color images

Trim: 8.5 x 11.75"
ISBN: 1-932026-77-1
US $120

Graphis Design 2013 features the most compelling design work of the year selected from hundreds of international entries. This volume includes Platinum award – winning entries from **Alt Group**, **GQ Magazine**, **Turner Duckworth**, **Strømme Throndsen Design** and **White Studio**. All published entries are presented on a spread with a case study description written by each designer or design firm.

Branding 6

2013
Hardcover: 256 pages
200-plus color images

Trim: 8.5 x 11.75"
ISBN: 1-932026-78-8
US $120

This book presents interviews, company profiles and visual histories of some of the biggest names in design and retail today, including: Q&A with **Pentagram**, **WAX**, **People design**, **Cue**, **Firewood**, **The General Design Co.**, **Studio International**, and **Alt Group**. All that, plus hundreds of images from the year's Graphis Gold Award-winning branding campaigns. This is a must-have for anyone interested in successful, creative branding – designers, businesses, students and fans alike.

Photography Annual 2013

2013
Hardcover: 256 pages
200-plus color images

Trim: 8.5 x 11.75"
ISBN:1-931241-80-1
US $120

Photography 2013 is a moving collection of the years best photographs. Shot by some of the world's respected photographers and selected from an international pool of entries, these beautifully reproduced images are organized by category for easy referencing. This year's book includes an interview with photographer **Bill Diadato**, discussing his background and the inspiration behind his work.

Masters of the 20th Century

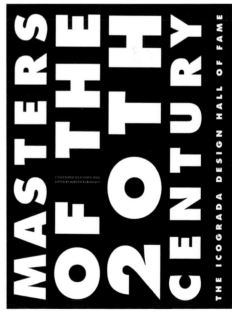

2012
Hardcover: 360 pages
200-plus color illustrations

Trim: 10 x 12"
ISBN: 1-888001-85-2
US $70

This is a huge volume that features the work and biographies of more than 100 top designers worldwide. Designed and edited by **Mervyn Kurlansky**, with distinct profiles of **Pierre Bernard**, **Wolfgang Weingart** and many others. A testament to exceptional talents and proof that they'll be remembered for generations to come, this book comes complete with a companion CD-ROM containing hundreds of additional images. Forewards by **Steven Heller** and **Marion Wesel-Henrion**.

Turbocharge your creativity with Graphis products.